Poison Ivy

This weed (above) causes an itchy rash if you touch it. Poison ivy grows as a vine or shrub. Try to remember what the leaves look like, and do not touch them or other parts of the plant. If you do touch poison ivy, washing your hands as soon as possible may reduce the itching. Your local drugstore will have various remedies that will help.

World Book's

SCIENCE & NATURE GUIDES

WILD FLOWERS

OF THE UNITED STATES AND CANADA

World Book, Inc.
a Scott Fetzer company
Chicago

Conservation

No flower grows in isolation from its surroundings. Each plant is part of a web of thousands of other plants and animals that live together. Different plants grow in different kinds of soil and climates. As you learn more about a habitat, you will get to know which flowers you could expect to find there.

Many habitats have been damaged or destroyed by pollution, agriculture, and industry. Some wild flowers are in danger of disappearing altogether because so many of their habitats have been disturbed or destroyed. On page 78, you will find the names of some organizations dedicated to the preservation of the countryside. By joining them and supporting their efforts, you can help to preserve our wild flowers and landscape.

As a general rule, do not pick flowers growing wild—you can study them just as easily where they are, and leave them to make seeds for next year's flowers. If you want to pick wild flowers, grow your own in a wilderness garden (see page 28). And, before you go walking in the country, make sure you read the Countryside Code below.

Countryside Code

1 **Always go walking with a friend,** and always tell an adult where you are going.

2 **Ask permission before exploring** or crossing private property.

3 **Keep to existing roads, trails, and pathways** wherever possible.

4 **Leave fence gates as you find them.**

5 **Only pick a wild flower** if you are sure it is common.

6 **Only pick one or two flowers** and then only from a large clump.

7 **Leave behind the roots** of flowers you pick and do not dig up bulbs or plants to take home.

8 **Keep out of crops** and do not walk on wild flowers.

This edition published in the United States of America by World Book, Inc., Chicago.

WORLD BOOK and the GLOBE DEVICE are registered trademarks or trademarks of World Book, Inc.

World Book, Inc.
233 North Michigan Avenue
Chicago, IL 60601 USA

For information about other World Book publications, visit our Web site **http://www.worldbook.com,** or call **1-800-WORLDBK (967-5325).** For information about sales to schools and libraries, call **1-800-975-3250 (United States); 1-800-837-5365 (Canada).**

Copyright © 2005 Chrysalis Children's Book Group, an imprint of Chrysalis Books Group Plc
The Chrysalis Building, Bramley Road, London, W10 6SP
www.chrysalis.com

Library of Congress Cataloging-in-Publication Data

Wild flowers of the United States and Canada.
  p. cm. — (World Book's science & nature guides)
  "Edited text and captions based on Wild flowers of North America by Pamela Forey"—T.p. verso.
  Includes bibliographical references and index.
  ISBN 0-7166-4220-4 — ISBN 0-7166-4208-5 (set)
  1. Wild flowers—United States—Identification. 2. Wild flowers—Canada—Identification. 3. Wild flowers—United States—Pictorial works. 4. Wild flowers—Canada—Pictorial works. I.Title: Wild flowers of the United States and Canada. II. Forey, Pamela. Wild flowers of North America. III. Series.

QK115 .W56 2005
582.13'097—dc22
                                    2004041914

Edited text and captions based on Wild Flowers of North America by Pamela Forey. Species illustrations by Norman Barber, Angela Beard, Richard Bell, Alma Hathaway, Roger Kent, David More, Susanna Stuart-Smith and David Thelwell, all of Bernard Thornton Artists, London. Habitat paintings and headbands by Antonia Phillips; identification and activities illustrations by Richard Coombes.

For World Book:
General Managing Editor: Paul A. Kobasa
Editorial: Shawn Brennan, Maureen Liebenson, Christine Sullivan
Research: Madolynn Cronk, Lynn Durbin, Cheryl Graham,
    Karen McCormack, Loranne Shields, Hilary Zawidowski
Librarian: Jon Fjortoft
Permissions: Janet Peterson
Graphics and Design: Sandra Dyrlund, Anne Fritzinger
Indexing: Aamir Burki, David Pofelski
Pre-press and Manufacturing: Carma Fazio, Steve Hueppchen,
    Jared Svoboda, Madelyn Underwood
Text Processing: Curley Hunter, Gwendolyn Johnson
Proofreading: Anne Dillon

Printed in China
1 2 3 4 5 6 7 8 9 10 09 08 07 06 05 04

Contents

Entries *like this* indicate pages featuring projects you can do!

Introduction To Wild Flowers

There are thousands of different wild flowers in North America. Not only are they beautiful, but many are useful, too. You might be surprised at how many have been used in herbal medicines for hundreds of years.

But some are extremely poisonous. You should never eat anything—flowers, leaves, seeds, or fruits—that you find growing wild. The chance of making a mistake is too great.

Being able to identify wild flowers is useful as well as fun. But, with so many different flowers that you might find, where do you start?

This book shows only the flowers you are most likely to see. It organizes them according to the habitat, or environment, where you are most likely to see them, then by flower color groups within each habitat. Habitats described in this book range from forests to deserts.

The life of a plant

Look for plants at all stages of their life cycles, as buds and fruits as well as flowers. Dandelions are called annuals—they die after producing seeds. To find out more about how plants reproduce and about pollination, see pages 18–19.

Biennials are plants that live for two growing seasons and perennials are ones that live for more than two growing seasons or even longer. Many perennials grow from bulbs (see page 28) or bulblike structures that give them a store of food that lasts through the winter.

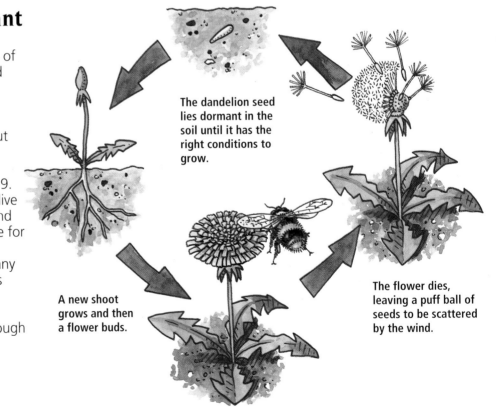

The dandelion seed lies dormant in the soil until it has the right conditions to grow.

The flower dies, leaving a puff ball of seeds to be scattered by the wind.

A new shoot grows and then a flower buds.

When the flower opens, insects move the pollen from the stamens to the stigma of the flower and the seeds are fertilized.

How to use this book

To identify a flower you do not recognize—for example, the climbing pink and the delicate white flowers shown here—follow these steps.

1 **Decide what habitat (environment) you are in.** Read the descriptions at the start of each section.

2 **What color is the flower?** In the section for the habitat you are in, look for the flowers with that color. The pictures and descriptions can help you identify your flower. The pink flower is field bindweed (on page 67).

3 **If you still can't find the flower,** look for it under another color subsection. Some flowers vary in color. White clover, for example, can have white or pink flowers.

4 **If you can't find the flower in the habitat you are in,** look through other habitats for flowers of that color. Some flowers grow in more than one kind of habitat. The white flower is wild carrot (on page 65).

5 **If you still can't find the flower,** you may have to look in a larger field guide. You may have found something that is very rare!

Top-of-page Picture Bands

Each section has a different picture band at the top of the page. These bands are shown below.

Eastern Forests

Grasslands

Western Forests

Wetlands

Deserts

Roadsides & Parks

What To Look For

Parts of a flower

The shapes of flowers and the color of their petals may be very different from one kind of plant to another, but all flowers have the same parts and fulfill the same purpose. They make seeds so that the plant can reproduce itself. To do this the male pollen has to fertilize the female ovules.

Members of the daisy family, among others, have a lot of tiny flowers packed into one composite flower head.

These straplike petals are really tiny flowers called ray flowers.

Each disk flower has its own ovary.

The center of this daisy is made up of tiny flowers called disk flowers.

The sepals protect the flower when it is a bud.

The ovary, stigma, and style are the female parts of the flower. The ovary contains eggs. When they are fertilized by the pollen, they grow into seeds.

Inside the bud, a new flower is forming.

The stamens are the male part of the flower. The anthers at the ends of the stems contain pollen.

This is the stigma. Pollen that catches on the stigma makes its way down the style to fertilize the eggs in the ovary.

Brightly colored petals attract insects to the flower.

The stem holds the plant up and carries food to all parts of the plant.

The plant's green leaves make food for the whole plant.

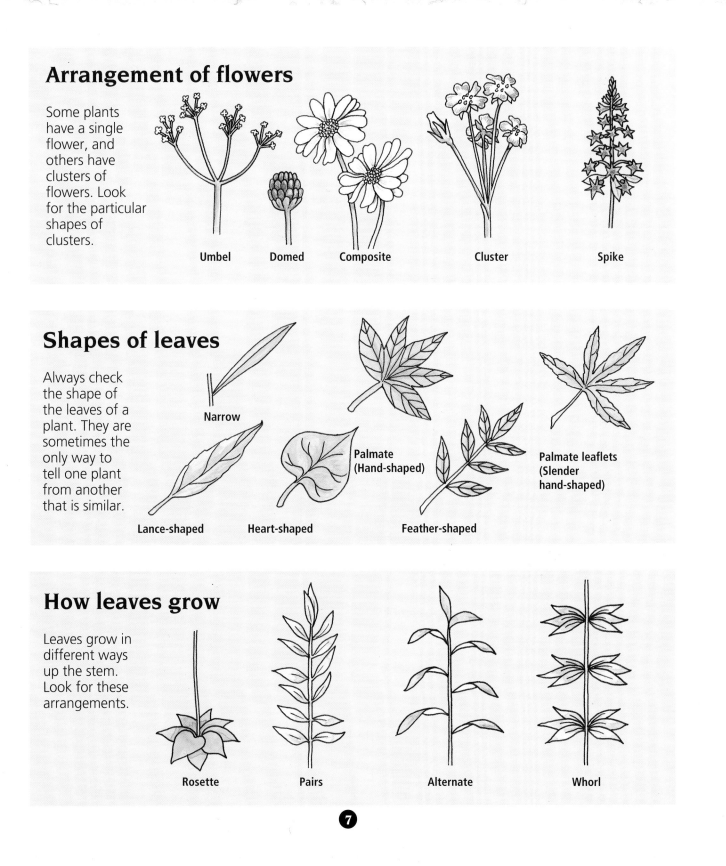

Arrangement of flowers

Some plants have a single flower, and others have clusters of flowers. Look for the particular shapes of clusters.

Umbel   **Domed**   **Composite**   **Cluster**   **Spike**

Shapes of leaves

Always check the shape of the leaves of a plant. They are sometimes the only way to tell one plant from another that is similar.

Narrow

Palmate (Hand-shaped)

Palmate leaflets (Slender hand-shaped)

Lance-shaped   **Heart-shaped**   **Feather-shaped**

How leaves grow

Leaves grow in different ways up the stem. Look for these arrangements.

Rosette   **Pairs**   **Alternate**   **Whorl**

Eastern Forests

There are several kinds of eastern forests, each with its own kinds of plants and flowers. The forests of the northern Great Lakes area and the northeast contain beech, birch, fir, maple, and spruce trees. Farther south you will find oaks and hickories. Along the southeastern coasts are the southern pine forests.

As you climb up a mountain, the forest changes in just the same way as if you were moving from south to north. All forests provide similar opportunities and problems for plants and flowers. Trees need a lot of water, so forests grow only where there is plenty of rain. Rotting leaves keep the soil fertile and damp.

But plants also need sunlight and trees keep the ground cool and shady. Look for most woodland flowers in the spring. These flowers race to grow, flower, and fruit before the trees get their leaves and block out most of the sunshine. Most are perennials, growing year after year from bulbs, rhizomes, or tubers—swollen underground stems or roots that store enough food and energy to last the plant until the next spring.

In the late spring and summer you will still find flowers in the forest, but look for most of them where more sunlight filters through—along paths, in clearings, and on the edge of the forest. The picture shows seven kinds of flowers from this section. How many can you identify?

Coral honeysuckle, Indian pipe, Jack-in-the-pulpit, smooth Solomon's-seal, starflower, purple trillium, yellow lady's-slipper

Mayapple

Don't touch a mayapple. It's poisonous and can irritate your skin. You are most likely to see it as a carpet of leaves covering the ground. Each stem has one or two large, umbrellalike leaves that have deep lobes. The flowers usually grow on stems with two leaves. The flowers are white and waxy. After they die, the plant develops berries, which become yellow when ripe.

Barberry family
12–18 in (30–46 cm) tall
Flowers in April–June
Also grows on shady roadsides

Wild Sarsaparilla

The round, greenish-white flowers of the wild sarsaparilla grow in a ball-shaped cluster at the end of a long flower stalk. The leaves grow on long stalks, too. They have three sections, each divided into leaflets. The fruits are dark blue-black berries. Wild sarsaparilla grows from an underground stem, or rhizome, which Native Americans brewed to make tea or root beer, or made into a stimulating medicine.

Ginseng family
6–20 in (15–51 cm) tall
Flowers in June–August

Wintergreen

These small, white flowers look like bells drooping from the base of the leaves. Look for this plant in the winter, too. The leaves are evergreen, and the berries, which ripen in the late summer, often stay on the plant all winter. Oil of wintergreen is used to flavor cough drops, toothpaste, and candy. The plant is sometimes called checkerberry or teaberry.

Heath family
Creeping stem with branches
2–6 in (5–15 cm) tall
Flowers in April–May
Also grows on mountainsides

Starflower

Look for these delicate starlike flowers in the cool, peaty woods across Canada and in much of the eastern United States. Each stem has two to three flowers, which grow on short stalks from the center of a whorl of five or six, dark green, shiny leaves. The petals have golden-yellow anthers.
Primrose family
4–8 in (10–20 cm) tall
Flowers in May–August

Nodding Trillium

The single white flower of the nodding trillium hangs, or nods, underneath the leaves. The flower has three white petals and a long stalk. The three oval, pointed leaves grow in a whorl near the top of the stem. Several similar white flowers grow in the East but their flowers don't hang like those of nodding trillium.
Lily family
6–18 in (15–46 cm) tall—Flowers in March–June
Grows in damp woods

Partridgeberry

Look for this plant trailing on the ground. The tubular flowers are white or pink, and grow in pairs. Notice how they are joined at the base and grow from the base of the uppermost leaves. The shiny leaves are evergreen, and grow in pairs along the branching stems. The flowers are followed by red berries, which remain on the plant in the winter.
Madder family
Creeping stem
Flowers in June–July
Sometimes grown in gardens

Bloodroot

These white flowers grow from a stout underground stem, called a rhizome. The single leaves are blue-green, kidney-shaped, and deeply lobed. The rhizomes have a deep orange-red sap. The plant has been used as an herbal medicine to treat skin problems like eczema and ringworm, but less painful remedies are used now.
Poppy family
About 10 in (25 cm) tall
Flowers in March
Also grown in gardens

Eastern Forests

Smooth Solomon's-seal

Look for Solomon's-seal growing in the shade. The greenish-white flowers are shaped like bells. They grow in ones or twos along the arching stem at the base of each pair of leaves. The leaves are broad and oval. The flowers die, and blue-black berries grow in their place along the stems.
Lily family
Up to 3 ft (91 cm) tall—Flowers in May–June

Wild Oat

Lily family
Up to 1 ft (30 cm) tall
Flowers in May–June
Also grows in mountains in the South

The drooping creamy-yellow flowers of this delicate-looking plant are shaped like long, narrow bells and grow at the end of the stem. Notice how the stem grows straight and leafless out of the ground. Then it forks near the top into two leafy branches. The leaves are narrow and pointed. The stems grow from a slender, underground rhizome.

Red Baneberry

Be careful—the berries of the red baneberry are very poisonous if eaten! Its white flowers grow in thick clusters at the end of a long flower stalk. The petals soon fall, leaving behind many white stamens. Look at the leaves. They are very large and divided into several toothed leaflets, each about 2–3 inches (5–8 centimeters) long. The flowers are followed by clusters of poisonous red berries.

Buttercup family
1–2 ft (30–61 cm) tall
Flowers in May–July

Downy Yellow Violet

There are several kinds of yellow violet, and each has five yellow petals. You can tell this is the downy yellow violet because it is covered with soft hairs. Look carefully at the flowers. They should have purple-brown veins on the underside of the petal. The leaves are 2–5 inches (5–13 centimeters) wide. They are heart-shaped with large, rounded teeth along the edges.
Violet family
Up to 16 in (41 cm) tall
Flowers in May–June
Grows in damp or shady places

Bluebead

The bluebead is also known as the corn lily. It has a cluster of three to eight greenish-yellow flowers. They are shaped like bells and grow at the end of a long flowering stalk. They are followed by bluish berries. The glossy green leaves are oval and pointed. Notice how they curl at the base around the stem. Each plant has two to five leaves that grow from a knotty underground rhizome.
Lily family
Up to 15 in (38 cm) tall
Flowers in May–August
Also grows on southern mountainsides

Dutchman's-breeches

This plant gets its name from its flowers. Breeches are short pants tied under the knee, and these flowers look like breeches hanging upside down from the flower stalks. The flowers fade from yellow to white. Look at the clumps of leaves, too. They are gray-green and feathery. They grow in clumps each year from swollen underground roots, called tubers.
Fumitory family
About 6–12 in (15–30 cm) tall
Flowers in March–April
Also grown in gardens

Goatsbeard

You will easily see this tall plant. It gets its name from its plumes of pale yellow, fluffy flowers. Look at the leaves, too. They are up to 15 inches (38 centimeters) long and divided into leaflets. Each leaflet is oblong and pointed, and has a jagged edge.
Aster family
Up to 6 ft (1.8 m) tall
Flowers in May–July
Also grown in gardens

Eastern Forests

Yellow Lady's-slipper

Lady's-slippers are sometimes called moccasin flowers. Both names come from the shape of the flower, whose pouched lips look like a slipper. Look for the magenta spots inside the pouched, yellow lips. Look at the yellow-to-purple wavy sepals, too. One points up, and the other two point down. Notice how the ribbed, oval leaves grab the stem.

Orchid family
Up to 2 ft (61 cm) tall—Flowers in May–June
Also grows in swamps and other parts of North America

Indian Pipe

You can't mistake this strange-looking plant. Look for it in leaf trash in damp woodlands in the summer. It grows in clumps of white or pink-to-red fleshy stems. They each bend over at the top into a bell-like flower with a yellow center. The leaves are translucent and look like scales on the stem.

Heath family
Up to 10 in (25 cm) tall
Flowers in June–August
Also found in damp woods all over North America

Jack-in-the-pulpit

This tall plant has only one or two large leaves divided into three leaflets. You may not see the flower at first. It grows under the leaves and has an arching leafy hood. The hood is green with maroon to whitish streaks. Look under the hood to see the green-to-brown, clublike spike, called a spathe, covered with tiny flowers. They are followed by a cluster of scarlet or red-orange berries later in the season.

Arum family
1–3 ft (30–91 cm) tall
Flowers in March–April
Grows in wet woodlands

Clammy Groundcherry

This plant is sticky rather than clammy. The heart-shaped, toothed leaves are covered with sticky hairs. Look for the bell-shaped flowers that hang from the base of the leaf stalks. They are greenish-yellow with purple centers. They are followed by papery sacs which enclose the fruit—yellow tomatolike berries.
Potato family
Up to 3 ft (91 cm) tall—Flowers in June–September
Also grows in grasslands

Spring Beauty

The spring beauty is a delicate plant with a sweet smell. Its white, pink, or rose-colored flowers are striped with darker pink or purple veins and grow in a cluster at the top of the stem. Each one usually has only two leaves. They are long and narrow, and grow opposite each other halfway up. Several stems grow from one fleshy corm (underground stem) hidden underneath the ground.
Purslane family—About 1 ft (30 cm) tall
Flowers in the spring and early summer
Also found in fields and clearings

Nodding Onion

You can identify this plant by its leaves, which smell like onions when crushed. The nodding clusters of pale flowers appear around the middle of the summer, but the clumps of long, soft, narrow leaves start to grow in the early summer. The nodding onion belongs to the same family as wild leeks and garlics, and is one of the best for eating. The bulbs from which it grows are like cultivated onions, and the leaves are good in salads.
Lily family
Up to 2 ft (61 cm) tall
Flowers in July–August
Also found in grasslands

Round-lobed Hepatica

The flowers may be white, pink, or lavender-blue. Although they look like regular flowers, they have no petals, but six petallike sepals instead. This hepatica is named for its leaves, which are divided into three rounded lobes. People used to think the leaves looked like the shape of the human liver. Hepaticas are sometimes called liverleafs or liverworts, and were used unsuccessfully to treat liver diseases.
Buttercup family
4–6 in (10–15 cm) tall
Flowers in March–April

Eastern Forests

Wood Lily

The wood lily has reddish-orange flowers with dark spots that point up. The three petals and three petallike sepals have narrow bases. There are six long, reddish-orange stamens with large anthers. The plant's leaves are lance-shaped and grow in whorls of 3–8 leaves.

Lily family
1–3 ft (30–91 cm) tall
Flowers in June–August
Grows in dry woodlands

Canadian Lousewort

You can recognize this plant from the thick clusters of red or yellow flowers that grow at the top of the stems. Each flower has two lips. Look at the finely cut leaves, too. Canadian lousewort, like other louseworts, is partly a parasite. The plant's roots attach themselves to the roots of other plants and steal their water and nutrients.

Figwort family
6–18 in (15–46 cm) tall
Flowers in April–June
Also grows in grasslands

Bergamot Orange

These tall, bright red flower heads are hard to miss. Look for the reddish bracts under the flowers. Look at the flowers, too. Each has a longish tube and two lips. If you are lucky you might see a hummingbird sipping the nectar. The leaves are lance-shaped and toothed, and grow in pairs up the long stems. Oil of bergamot is produced from the plant and is used to flavor tea.

Mint family
Up to 5 ft (1.5 m) tall
Flowers in June–August
Also grows on mountainsides and in gardens

Purple Trillium

This deep red or maroon flower has three petals and three green sepals, which you can see in between the petals. The flower smells like rotting meat. This smell attracts flies that pollinate the flower. Its whorl of three diamond-shaped leaves grows at the top of the stem, underneath the flower.

Lily family
8–16 in (20–41 cm) tall
Flowers in April–June

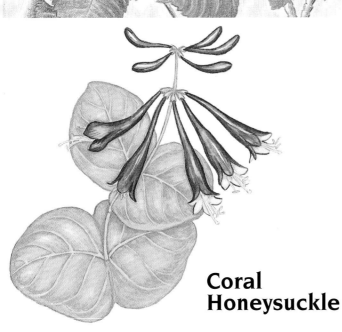

Fall Phlox

You will easily spot these showy, deep pink or lavender flowers. They grow in clusters at the end of a tall, leafy stem. The flowers are followed by capsules of seeds. The plant then dies, but grows up again the next year.
Phlox family
Up to 6 ft (1.8 m) tall
Flowers in August–October
Also grown in gardens

Coral Honeysuckle

This honeysuckle, also called the trumpet honeysuckle, is a climbing plant whose stems twine into the branches of shrubs and trees. You will easily see the whorls of brilliant colored, trumpet-shaped flowers. They are red on the outside and orange-yellow inside. They are rich in nectar and attract many insects and hummingbirds. Look at the pairs of oval leaves, too. Those underneath the flowers join across the stem to form a disk.
Honeysuckle family
Climbing vine—Flowers in April–August

Wild Columbine

These flowers are easy to recognize. The nodding red and yellow flowers are formed from red sepals and red and yellow petals. The nectar is inside the hollow "claws" of the petals. The delicate leaves are divided into groups of three leaflets.

Fire Pink

These crimson flowers often form large patches of color in open woods and rocky places. They grow in clusters at the ends of the weak stems. Look closely at one of the flowers. It has five narrow petals which grow from a long tube of sticky sepals. The leaves are long and narrow and grow in twos or fours.
Pink family
6–24 in (15–61 cm) tall
Flowers in April–June

Buttercup or crowfoot family
2–4 ft (61–121 cm) tall
Flowers in April–July
Also grows in rocky places

How Plants Make Seeds

Flowering plants produce eggs (known as ovules) in the female part of the flower (the ovary), and pollen grains in the male part of the flower (the anthers). If you don't know where these parts of the flower are, look at pages 6 and 7, which tell you what to look for. Pollen grains are carried from one flower to another by the wind, or by animals, usually insects.

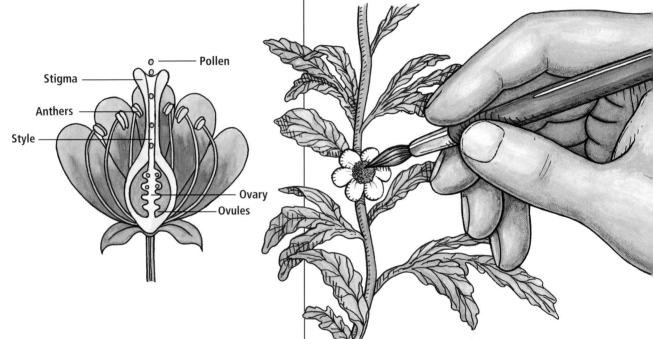

Pollen

Stigma

Anthers

Style

Ovary

Ovules

Insects are attracted to flowers by their bright petals, their scent, and their sweet-tasting nectar. As insects feed on the nectar and pollen, some pollen sticks to their bodies and is rubbed off on the next flower they visit.

If it is pollen from the same kind of flower, and if it sticks to the stigma, the pollen grows a tube to travel down the style into the ovary. There each grain of pollen joins with one ovule to fertilize it and produce a seed.

When most of the ovules have been fertilized by a pollen grain, the petals begin to wither and die. The seeds swell and grow in the ovary until they are ready to be scattered.

Pollinating a tomato plant

Only the right sort of pollen will fertilize the ovules. In this experiment, you are the pollinator. You will take the pollen from one flower and move it to another.

1 **Buy one or two tomato plants** and plant them in pots of compost. Use large pots, because the plants will grow up to 5 feet (1.5 meters) tall. Put them in a sunny place and water them regularly.

2 **When the flowers open,** you can use an artist's paintbrush to transfer pollen from one flower to another. Push the brush into the flower and gently wiggle it about. Then push the brush into another flower and do the same thing.

3 **To test whether the pollen from another flower will fertilize the ovules,** first collect pollen from a different kind of flower—a geranium or poppy for example—and pollinate one flower on the tomato plant. Tie a bit of thread loosely around its stalk so that you can remember which flower you used for this test.

4 **Now pollinate the other tomato flowers** with tomato pollen. Use a clean paintbrush every time you use a different sort of pollen.

5 **Carefully place a large, clear plastic bag over the plant** when you have finished pollinating, and tie it around the pot. This stops other pollens from reaching the flowers.

6 **As soon as the flowers wither,** you can take the plastic bag off.

7 **Which flowers develop into tomatoes?** The flowers with the thread around the stalk, which you pollinated with geranium pollen, should not. If they do, it is because they were already pollinated with tomato pollen beforehand.

Scattering seeds

Flowers use many different methods to spread their seeds as widely as possible. Dandelions produce many seeds, each with a "parachute," which is blown in the wind. Only a few will land where they can grow, but that is enough to ensure survival.

Some seeds have tiny hooks that cling to clothes or to the fur of animals. The seeds may drop from the clothing or fur and grow in the place where they fall.

Many seeds are wrapped in tasty berries that are snapped up by birds and other animals. The berries are eaten. But the seeds are dropped, or they may pass right through the animal's body and start to grow miles (or kilometers) from the parent flowers.

Lupines, vetches, and other members of the pea and bean family have pods of seeds that burst open when they are ripe and scatter their seeds in all directions.

Poppy heads explode to scatter their seeds.

Seeds with burrs stick to clothes or fur.

Dandelion seeds have their own "parachutes."

Berries are eaten or carried away by birds and animals.

Water lily seeds float away from their parent plant.

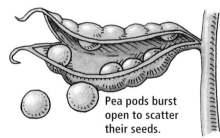

Pea pods burst open to scatter their seeds.

Grasslands

Grasslands get less rain than forests but more rain than deserts. Here you will find miles (or kilometers) of land covered with grasses and wild flowers. The flowers that grow in grasslands like full sunshine, so look for them in the late spring, summer, and fall.

Water is scarce on the grasslands. Much of the rain evaporates in the wind and sun. Wild flowers that grow here have found their own ways of getting and conserving water, like the large taproots that reach deep into the soil for water. Some are covered with dense white or silvery hairs. The hairs reflect some of the sun's rays and protect the plant from the drying wind.

The prairies are the largest grasslands in North America, but there are other grassland areas in the Southwest, California, and between the Rocky Mountains and the more western mountains of the Sierra Nevada and the Cascade Range.

The prairies change from shortgrass in the West, where there is less rain, to tall grass in the East, where more rain falls. Much of the tall grass prairie has been taken over for agriculture or by forests. Only isolated areas remain, such as along railroads. The picture shows seven kinds of flowers from this section. How many can you identify?

Hairy false goldenaster, tansy aster, wild blue flax, scarlet globe mallow, sego lily, American pasqueflower, western wallflower

Banana Yucca

You can't miss this tall, flowering stem with its many waxy, bell-like flowers. The flowers are creamy-white on the inside, but often tinged with purple on the outside. The flower heads grow from a clump of swordlike spine-tipped leaves about 3 feet (91 cm) high. The flowers are followed by edible fleshy pods, which taste like sweet potatoes when they are baked.

Agave family
Up to 5 ft (1.5 m) tall
Flowers in April–July
Also found in deserts and scrub

Sego Lily

This white flower is the state flower of Utah. It grows in clusters at the top of the stem. Look at the complicated yellow and red markings around the center of the petals. The leaves are long and narrow, and often roll upward at the edges. Like other mariposa lilies, it grows from a bulb.

Lily family
Up to 18 in (46 cm) tall
Flowers in May–July
Also grows in woods and sagebrush

Prairie Star

This plant has small, starlike flowers. Look closely at the white or pinkish petals. They are divided into three or five lobes. The flowers open just as the clumps of leaves at the base are emerging and growing larger. The leaves are lobed and hairy.

Saxifrage family
Up to 20 in (51 cm) tall
Flowers in March–June
Also grows in dry woods, in sagebrush, and on the lower slopes of the Rocky Mountains

Canadian Anemone

These white flowers grow at the end of a long stem. They don't have petals, but the five sepals look like petals. The leaves, like buttercup leaves, are palmate. Those at the base have long stalks. But look at those on the stem—they have no stalks at all. This is a sure way of identifying this plant. The flowering stems and leaves grow from long, underground stems.

Buttercup family
1–2 ft (30–61 cm) tall
Flowers in May–July
Also grows in meadows and thickets

Grasslands

Hairy False Goldenaster

The yellow flower heads of hairy false goldenaster grow in clusters at the ends of the stems. The center of each is yellow and, as the flower gets older, the surrounding yellow ray florets begin to roll underneath. Before the flowers appear, you may see the plant as mounds of gray, branched, leafy stems. The gray color comes from the small, lance-shaped leaves that are thickly covered with hairs.
Composite family
Up to 20 in (51 cm) tall
Flowers in May–October
Also found on roadsides and rocky hillsides

Rocky Mountain Zinnia

This bright yellow-orange flower is also called the little golden zinnia. It has a reddish central disk and only three to six round, yellow ray florets surrounding it. It grows in low clumps, and you may not see it until late summer, when it is suddenly covered with flower heads. The linear leaves grow in pairs up the branching stems.
Composite family
3–9 in (8–23 cm) tall
Flowers in June–October
Also grows in deserts

Common Sunflower

You can't miss these large yellow flower heads. Many measure more than 1 foot (30 centimeters) across. They are purplish-brown in the center surrounded by bright yellow ray florets. They grow on tall, branching, leafy stems. Look for the oval or triangular leaves. They are toothed and rough and grow up to 1 foot (30 centimeters) long. The seeds can be eaten like the ones from cultivated sunflowers.
Composite family
Up to 10 ft (3 m) tall—Flowers in July–September

Plains Prickly Pear

You will easily recognize prickly pears because of their long flattened stems. The stems are made up of oval sections that are 2 to 6 inches (5 to 15 centimeters) long. The flowers are yellow or red and are followed by prickly fruits. Wear thick gloves if you pick them. The flowers and stems have many fine bristles in between the tufts of long spines. These gray, woolly bristles will irritate your skin more than the spikes.

Cactus family
4–24 in (10–61 cm) tall
Flowers in May–June

Western Wallflower

Wallflowers are often seen growing in gardens, but the western wallflower is a spectacular wild variety. The flowers may be yellow, burnt-orange, or brick-red. They yield to slender, rectangular pods that grow straight up at first, then slope out from the stem. The leaves are lance-shaped and alternate up the stem.

Mustard family
Up to 3 ft (91 cm) tall
Flowers in March–July

Showy Gaillardia

You can't miss this bright, showy flower. It is also called firewheel because its outer reddish petals have yellow ends. Each flower head actually consists of two kinds of flowers—the tubular flowers in the disk and the ray flowers with long petals. Look for the three deep teeth in each ray. Notice how bristly the lobed leaves are.

Composite family
12–24 in (30–61 cm) tall
Flowers in May–July
Also grows on roadsides and in gardens

Cream Cups

These flowers vary in color from creamy-white to yellow, or white with yellow spots on the base of the petals. Like other poppies, they have many stamens in the center of the flower. Each plant has several hairy stems. The soft, hairy, linear leaves grow opposite each other on the lower half of the stem. Look for the fruit. The ovary separates into many sections that grow upward when the fruit forms.

Poppy family
4–12 in (10–30 cm) tall
Flowers in March–May

Grasslands

Old Man's Whiskers

This plant is also called prairie smoke because it looks like puffs of smoke when it has gone to seed. The flowers are reddish or pink, nodding, and urn-shaped. They yield to seeds with long, feathery hairs. The plant is hairy and has clumps of pinnate leaves at its base. Notice how the small leaflets alternate with large ones.

Rose family
6–16 in (15–41 cm) tall
Flowers in April–August
Also grows in mountain ridges

Sagebrush Mariposa Lily

Look for this unusual-shaped flower in much the same places as the sego lily (see page 21), to which it is closely related. The three broad, pink or lilac petals are marked with yellow hairs and a crescent of dark red. Notice the three narrow sepals between the petals which are longer than the petals. There are several narrow, grasslike leaves on the stem.

Lily family—6–24 in (15–61 cm) tall
Flowers in May–August
Also grows in woods
and sagebrush

Indian Paintbrush

The flowers are greenish-yellow, but are hardly seen at the base of the bright orange and scarlet, fan-shaped bracts. The flowers get their name from a Native American legend about a man who became frustrated while trying to paint a prairie sunset— the great spirit made these flowers spring up where he threw down his brushes. The leaves alternate up the stem and are divided into several narrow lobes.

Figwort family
12–24 in (30–61 cm) tall
Flowers in May–July

Queen of the Prairie

You can't miss these large, fluffy, pink clumps. Look closely to see how they are made up of sprays of tiny, sweet-scented flowers. Look at the dark green leaves, too. They are pinnate with many toothed leaflets. This flower is less common in the East and South, where any you see have probably escaped from yards.

Rose family
3 to 6 ft
(0.9–1.8 m) tall
Flowers in
June–August
Also grown
in gardens

Showy Evening Primrose

As its name tells you, this flower opens only in the evening. During the day you will see only the white or pink, nodding buds. The flowers grow from the base of the leaves, which are lance-shaped and have shallow lobes. You might also see this plant east of the prairies, growing in empty lots and along roadsides.
Evening primrose family
Up to 2 ft (61 cm) tall
Flowers in May–July
Also grown in gardens

Rough Blazing Star

You can't miss these long spikes of bright purple, fluffy flower heads. Unusually, the flower heads open from the top of the spike downward. Each one grows from the base of a leaf. The leaves are narrow and grow in a clump at the base of the stem, and then alternate up the stem. Blazing stars are also called gayfeathers, because of their fluffy appearance.
Composite family
1–4 ft (30–121 cm) tall
Flowers in August–October
Also found in open woods

Scarlet Globe Mallow

These brick-red or reddish-orange flowers grow in spikes at the end of the weak stems, which are covered with soft, velvety hairs. Those at the bottom of the spike open first. Look for the fruits. They grow in a circle and are also covered with hairs. The leaves are rounded and have deep lobes. The stems grow from a woody taproot.
Mallow family
Up to 20 in (51 cm) tall
Flowers in April–August
Also grows on roadsides

Grasslands

Tansy Aster

This plant has a lot of flower heads, each with a yellow central disk surrounded by blue-purple petals. To be sure that it is a tansy aster, check its leaves. They are divided and look like the leaves of a tansy (see page 71). The plant is sometimes called tahoka daisy.

Composite family
4–16 in (10–41 cm) tall
Flowers in May-September

Lambert Crazyweed

Look for the bright pink or lavender flower clusters standing up above the leaves. Look at the tufts of leaves, too. Each leaf has 11 to 17 narrow leaflets covered with silvery, silky hairs. The flowers are followed by plump, oblong, pointed seed pods that stand up. Like many other locoweeds, this plant is well known to be poisonous to sheep and cattle.

Pea family
Up to 15 in (38 cm) tall
Flowers in April–July

American Pasqueflower

This is the state flower of South Dakota. It is a small plant, and it is thickly covered with hairs. The flowers are purple, lavender, or blue with yellow stamens. They grow from the end of a long stalk. They are followed by clumps of deeply cut leaves. As the flowers die and the fruits ripen, the seeds develop long, feathery tips.

Crowfoot family
Up to 15 in (38 cm) tall
Flowers in May–August

Leadplant

You can't miss these thick, blue flower heads. Look closely at the flowers. They each have only one blue petal and 10 bright orange stamens. The leaves are divided into 15 to 45 crowded leaflets. They are covered with white hairs, making them look gray. The flowers are followed by seed pods that are also hairy.

Pea family
Up to 3 ft (91 cm) tall
Flowers in May–August

Silverleaf Indian Breadroot

This plant looks silvery due to the silky white hairs that cover it. The tiny flowers are very dark blue, but their sepals have silver hairs. They grow in small clusters on long stalks rising from the upper leaves. The leaves are divided into three to five oval leaflets. The flowers are followed by silky pods that contain one seed each. It is also called silverleaf scurfpea.
Pea family
Up to 2 ft (61 cm) tall
Flowers in June–August

Harvest Brodiaea

Look for these clusters of reddish-purple or purple flowers growing on bare stalks that grow upward. Notice how the petals join to make a funnel-shaped flower. You won't see the grassy leaves because they have already withered before the flowers open. The leaves and flowering stems grow each year from a short underground stem called a corm.
Lily family
Up to 20 in (51 cm) tall
Flowers in April–July
Grows in California and Oregon

Five-spot

Notice how these pale blue flowers are almost white at the center. They can measure over 1 inch (2.5 centimeters) across and are shaped like bowls. They grow on thin stalks near the ends of the stems. Look for the compound leaves divided into pinnate, toothed leaflets, too. The stems are thin and branched. The flowers are followed by capsules of seeds.
Waterleaf family
6–12 in (15–30 cm) tall
Flowers in March–April
Also found on hillsides, sage scrub, chaparral, and near the West Coast

Wild Blue Flax

You can recognize this plant from its loose clusters of sky-blue flowers and a lot of tiny, erect leaves that alternate up its stems. Look closely at the flowers. Each has five petals and five sepals. Wild blue flax is related to common flax, which is grown commercially and made into linseed oil and linen.
Flax family
½–2½ ft (15–76 cm) tall
Flowers in May–July
Also grown in gardens

Growing Wild Flowers

Instead of picking flowers from the wild, why not grow your own in pots, window boxes, or in your yard? Look for packets of wild-flower seeds in your local garden center. When the seeds flower, you can pick as many as you'd like.

Creating a wilderness

Birds and insects love weeds and wild plants. Ask your parents if you can make a special corner of your yard into a wilderness. Let the grass grow and soon you will have dandelions, buttercups, clover, and other common flowers growing there, too.

Whatever you do, don't weed it! Buy a packet of wild-flower seeds and scatter them there as well. Leave any fallen leaves to rot. Put some old logs and big stones in there, too.

Then wait and watch. Wood lice and various insects will soon move in on the old leaves and logs. Birds will come to feed on the insects. In the summer, bumble bees, butterflies, and other insects will pollinate the flowers.

Keep a record of the flowers that grow and the animals that visit. If you can, make a small pond and grow water plants in it. You may soon find tadpoles and frogs in there, too. **Do not make a pond in an area where small children play. Do not make a pond if you live in an area prone to West Nile virus.**

Grow flowers from bulbs

Many of the earliest spring flowers grow from bulbs. The bulb is a store of food that lets the plant shoot up and grow before it is warm enough for most flowers.
Only use bulbs that you can buy—never dig up bulbs that are growing wild.

1 **Buy your bulbs in the fall** and plant them in pots of compost, or garden soil mixed with sand. Dampen the compost before you begin.
2 **Half fill the pot with soil or compost,** then plant the bulbs with the pointed end upward. Leave about 1 inch (2.5 centimeters) between them. Cover them with soil until only the tips show.
3 **Leave the bulbs in a dark, airy place** until they begin to grow. Don't forget about them and be sure to keep the compost damp.
4 **You should see the first shoots** in about two months. Put the pots in a warm, sunny place and water them. Try planting seeds from apples or oranges, and the pits from avocados or peaches, as well. Plant them as described above, put them on a window sill, and keep them well watered.

Hidden seeds

You can grow a surprise garden from the seeds you pick up on your sneakers on a muddy walk. **Be sure to wash your hands well after handling the mud.**

1 **Put on your sneakers and take a walk** with an adult after rain. Walk along the side of a garden or other muddy place, such as a forest.

2 **Scrape the mud from your sneakers** when you get home, and put it in a clean jar or plastic container. Mix in enough water with the mud to make it runny and leave the mixture to soak overnight.

3 **Ask an adult to heat the oven to 400 °F (200 °C)** while you half fill an old metal or disposable tray or baking dish with garden soil or compost. Bake the soil for 30 minutes. This will kill any seeds that are in it already. Leave it to cool in the oven overnight.

4 **Alternatively,** you can buy sterile compost from a garden center.

5 **The next day, add the mud and water mixture** to the baked soil. Cover the tray with a sheet of clear plastic and store it in a warm place.

6 **The seedlings will begin to grow** after two or three weeks. As they get larger, carefully move them to bigger pots in a sunny place, so you can watch them grow to full size. Throw the tray away.

7 **Can you identify all the plants?** Use this book to help you name them.

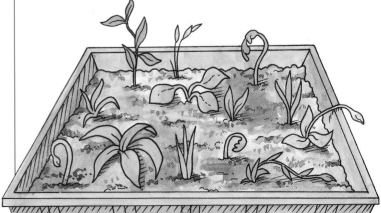

Western Forests

Most western forests are made up of evergreen trees with needlelike leaves, such as pines, spruces, and firs. Different kinds of forests have different wild flowers growing in them. With a little practice, you will learn which flowers you could expect to find in a lodgepole pine forest, an Engelmann spruce forest, a ponderosa pine forest, and so on.

Some western forests have deciduous trees, such as aspens. Here, as in eastern forests (see pages 8 to 17), you will find most flowers in spring, when sunlight can warm the soil before the new leaves emerge.

Which trees and flowers grow in a forest depends on the amount of rain and sunshine the forest receives. Damp air from the Pacific Ocean blows across the mountains and valleys from west to east. The western sides of the mountain slopes are wetter than the eastern slopes. In some places the eastern mountainsides may be too dry for trees to grow at all—there is grassland and then desert.

Mountainsides that face south get more sun. So you are most likely to find trees and flowers that like a cool, wet environment on the northwestern side of a mountain, and those that like warmer and drier conditions on the southeastern side. This picture shows eight kinds of flowers from this section. How many can you identify?

Orange agoseris, Colorado blue columbine, yellow dogtooth violet, bush beardtongue, western shooting star, western rattlesnake plantain, heartleaf arnica, blue-pod lupine

Tall Cinquefoil

Look for the cluster of white flowers growing at the top of a thick stem that grows upward. Each flower has five petals cupped in two sets of sepals. Look for the other set of sepals below the top set. Feel the leaves and stem. They are covered with sticky, brown hairs. The leaves are divided into 7 to 11 toothed, oval leaflets.
Rose family
Up to 3 ft (91 cm) tall
Flowers in May–August
Also grows in grasslands and is found farther east to Arizona

Tassel-flower Brickellbush

Look for this plant in rocky places. The nodding flower heads are pale yellow or greenish, and grow in clusters on short stalks from the base of a leaf. They look like the center of daisies cupped in green-and-yellow striped bracts. Look for the triangular leaves that grow in pairs up the stem, too.
Composite family
1 to 3 ft (30–91 cm) tall
Flowers in July–October
Also grows on cliffs and mountainsides

Richardson's Geranium

Look for this plant in damp woods. It grows from a clump of leaves, each of which is deeply cut into five to seven sections. The flowers are white or pinkish and have purple veins. Look for the fruits when the flowers have died. Each fruit has five spoon-shaped sections with a seed in the bowl of each "spoon." When the seeds are ripe, the spoon handles contract and pull the bowls upward, throwing out the seeds.
Geranium family
Up to 2½ ft (76 cm) tall
Flowers in June–August
Also grows in meadows

Miner's Lettuce

This unusual-looking plant likes damp and shady places. At the end of each flowering stem is a broad bowl-shaped disk, formed from two leaves that have joined together around the stem. In the center of each disk is a cluster of small, white flowers. Look for the clumps of spoon-shaped leaves. They are rich in vitamin C and gold miners used to eat them like lettuce.

Purslane family
Up to 1 ft (30 cm) tall
Flowers in March–July

White Inside-out Flower

You will easily recognize the strange shape of this flower. Both the white petals and sepals are swept back so that the flowers look like they are inside-out. The leaves are divided into groups of three leaflets, each with three lobes. They grow from underground rhizomes and form a slow-spreading carpet on the shady forest floor.

Barberry family
Up to 20 in (51 cm) tall
Flowers in May–July

Western Rattlesnake Plantain

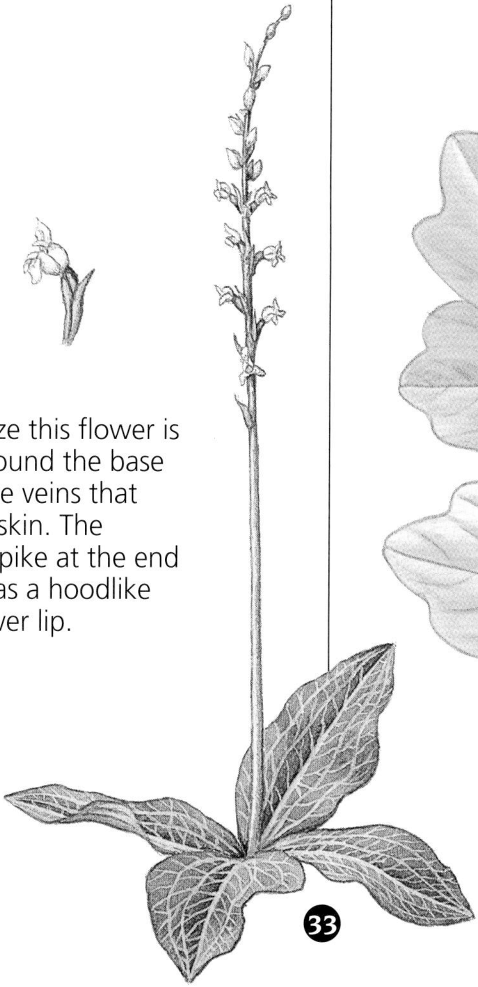

The easiest way to recognize this flower is by its leaves. They grow around the base of the stem, and have white veins that make them look like snakeskin. The whitish flowers grow in a spike at the end of the stem. Each flower has a hoodlike upper lip and a cupped lower lip.

Orchid family
Up to 1½ ft (46 cm) tall
Flowers in May–September

Orange Agoseris

This plant looks a lot like a dandelion except that its flowers are a striking burnt-orange instead of yellow. As they get older, they turn purple or deep pinkish. The orange agoseris is one of about 10 mountain dandelions. Like real dandelions, they have long, toothed leaves and flower stems full of milky juice.

Composite family
Up to 2 ft (61 cm) tall
Flowers in June–August

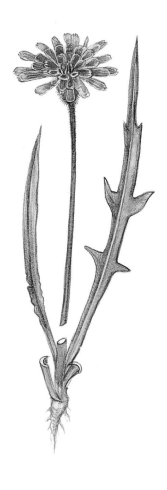

Heartleaf Arnica

Look for large patches of heartleaf arnica in open woods. It has one, two, or three yellow flower heads growing at the end of the stems. Look for the pairs of heart-shaped leaves, too. Like European arnica, this plant has been used in herbal medicine to treat bruises and strains, but it can irritate the skin. It is poisonous if eaten.

Composite family
1 to 2 ft (30–61 cm) tall
Flowers in April–June

Nuttall's Violet

Also known as the prairie yellow violet, these yellow flowers have five petals, often tinged with purple on the outside. Look for the brownish-purple veins on the petals. The flowers look a lot like the downy yellow violet (see page 12), but their leaves are very different. They are lance-shaped or oval.

Violet family
2–5 in (5–13 cm) tall
Flowers in April
Also grows in grasslands

Summer Coralroot

Look carefully at these yellowish or purple flowering stalks. They don't have any leaves, only a few sheaths near their base. Look at the flowers, too. Their sepals and side petals are almost the same color as the stalk, but the lip is whitish and spotted with purple. Coralroots grow from an underground rhizome that looks like coral. They get their food from a special fungus that grows with them. This plant is also called spotted coralroot.

Orchid family
6–20 in (15–15 cm) tall
Flowers in July–September

Yellow Dogtooth Violet

Yellow dogtooth violet blooms as the snows begin to melt. This flower grows from corms (food-rich underground stems) and forms large patches of many plants. Look for the two oval or lance-shaped leaves at the base of each stem and for one to five nodding yellow flowers. Dogtooth violets are also called adder's-tongues from the way the stamens flick out from the swept-back petals.

Lily family
6–12 in (15–30 cm) tall
Flowers in March–August
Also found on grassy slopes and grown in gardens

Western Forests

Scarlet Gilia

This plant has a lot of other names—they all tell you something about it. Some people call it skunk flower because of its light smell of skunk. Others call it scarlet gilia and foxfire for the color of the flowers. These flowers are usually bright red, mottled with yellow, but can be pink. Still other people call this flower desert trumpet or skyrocket for the way the petals form a tube bent back at the ends. The leaves are deeply dissected into narrow segments, and grow mostly lower on the stems.
Phlox family
1–7 ft (0.3–2.1 m) tall
Flowers in May–September
Also grows in scrub, chaparral, and yards

Beard-lip Beardtongue

You can't miss these bright red, showy flowers. They form a clump of thin stems that grow upward, and end with many drooping flowers growing from them on short stalks. The petals form a tube that ends in two lips. The lower lip has yellow hairs near the tip. The leaves are long and grasslike. This plant is also known as southwestern penstemon.
Figwort family
Up to 3 ft (91 cm) tall
Flowers in June–September
Also grown in yards

Manzanita

Manzanita is the Spanish American name for this plant. Europeans call it bearberry. It is a woody, shrubby plant that grows close to the ground and often covers large areas. Look for the white or pink, bell-shaped flowers. They are followed by bright red berries. Look for the spoon-shaped evergreen leaves, too. The Native Americans used to smoke them like tobacco. The leaves also were used for tanning leather.

Heath family
Creeping stem up to 10 ft (3 m) long and 6 in (15 cm) tall
Flowers in March–June
Grows in sandy and rocky ground

Western Shooting Star

You can't mistake this unusual and beautiful flower. Look for the drooping clusters of magenta (purplish red) flowers. Each has white bands and is shaped like a dart. Notice how the stamens are joined together and form a beak shape and the petals are swept back. The flower stem grows from a rosette of lance-shaped or oval leaves.
Primrose family
6–24 in (15–61 cm) tall
Flowers in May–September
Also found on grassland, coasts, and in yards

Fritillary

These flowers, which vary in color, look checkered or mottled. They are shaped like bowls and hang on arching stems from the base of the leaves. The leaves are lance-shaped and grow in whorls of three to five leaves. The thin stems grow upward from small bulbs.

Lily family
Up to 4 ft (1.2 m) tall
Flowers in March–April
Also grows in scrub

Pipsissewa

Look for these waxy, fragrant flowers in early and middle summer. Four to eight white or pinkish flowers hang from the top of each stem. They each have 5 petals and 10 stamens with dark pink or red anthers. The narrow leaves are toothed and leathery, and they grow in whorls on the stem. The plant was used by many Native Americans as an herbal remedy for rheumatism and kidney stones.

Shinleaf family
Up to 1 ft (30 cm) tall
Flowers in June–August
Also grows in forests in southern Canada and much of the U.S.

Nettleleaf Giant Hyssop

This flower is easy to spot because of the thick spike of flowers that grows at the ends of the upward-growing stems. See how the flower head is made up of whorls of pale pink or lavender flowers, and how the stamens stick out beyond the flowers. The leaves look a lot like nettles—another name for the plant is nettleleaf horsemint.

Mint family
Up to 5 ft (1.5 m) tall
Flowers in June–August

Western Forests

Showy Polemonium

This plant, also called showy Jacob's ladder, has 11 to 23 pale green leaflets arranged in pairs opposite each other so that they look like a ladder. Crush one so you can smell its skunklike scent. The flowers, which grow in clusters at the ends of the stems, are blue with yellow throats, and shaped like bowls.

Phlox family
2–12 in (5–30 cm) tall
Flowers in May–August
Grows all over the higher western mountains

Western Dog Violet

The flowers of the western dog violet vary in color from pale to dark violet. They have five petals, and the upper two are bent upward. Look for the backward spur on the lowest petal. Look at the leaves, too. They are rounded and scalloped around the edge. The stalk is long and erect.

Violet family
Up to 8 in (20 cm) tall
Flowers in March–July
Also found in meadows and on hillsides

Helmet Flower

Helmet flowers are easy to recognize. Make sure you don't touch them because they are very poisonous. A lot of showy flowers, often blue-violet in color, grow on each stem. The sepals look like petals and the top one forms a helmet-shaped hood over the flower. The large leaves are toothed and deeply lobed. It is also called western monkshood or aconite.

Crowfoot family
Up to 6 ft (1.8 m) tall
Flowers in June–August
Also grows in high meadows

Blue-pod Lupine

You will easily spot these long thick flower heads. Most of them are violet or blue, but some have reddish flowers. Notice how the sides of the petals are bent back, giving the typical pealike flower that yields to pods of seeds. The leaves are large, compound, and palmate, with leaflets arranged almost like spokes on a wagon wheel. This is the only lupine to grow in damp, lush places. Garden lupines have been developed from it.

Pea family
Up to 5 ft (1.5 m) tall
Flowers in June–August
Also grows in damp meadows and next to streams

Colorado Blue Columbine

The Colorado blue columbine is the state flower of Colorado. It is easy to recognize because of its large, blue sepals and scoop-shaped, white petals that extend backward into hollow, blue claws that hold the nectar. The flowers are followed by clusters of five segmented pods. The leaves are delicate and compound with deeply lobed leaflets, and grow in clumps.

Crowfoot family
Up to 3 ft (91 cm) tall
Flowers in May–August
Grows in the Rocky Mountains

Bush Beardtongue

This low-growing, shrubby plant forms thick patches of branching woody stems. Look for the showy lavender flowers and the pairs of lance-shaped leaves. Many flowers grow on each stem. The five petals join together to form a long tube, with a two-lobed upper lip and a three-lobed lower lip, that flares out at the end.

Figwort family
No more than 15 in (38 cm) tall
Flowers in June–August
Grows on damp, rocky slopes; also grown in rock gardens

Experiments with Plants

Everyone knows plants need water and light, or they will die. They take in water from the soil through their roots. But how does water flow up from the roots to every other part of a plant? Perform an experiment to find out how. Also, perform experiments to show plants turning to the light, and making water and oxygen.

Coloring a flower

This experiment shows how stems move water from the roots to the leaves and flowers.

1 **Take a white flower**—like a carnation, geranium, or wild carrot (see page 65)—and carefully split the lower part of its stem into two.
2 **Fill two small pots with water.** Color one with red food dye and the other with blue or another color.
3 **Put one half of the stem** in one pot and the other half in the other pot. Prop or tape the flower upright. Leave it for an hour or two, or overnight.
4 **What happens to the flower?** Look at the split stem to see the tiny tubes, or "xylem," now colored by the dyed water.

You can use any color food dye in these pots. Or you can mix two colors together (red and blue, for example, to make purple). But be careful—don't spill any on your clothes!

Plants lose water, too

Plants breathe just like we do. They take in oxygen from the air through tiny holes in their leaves. These holes are called "stomata." Plants need both oxygen and food to grow. As the oxygen and sugar (food) are broken down, they give off carbon dioxide and water, which leave through the stomata.

1 **Take a small potted plant** and water it well.
2 **Put a clear plastic bag over all the leaves.** Make sure your bag is large enough so that it doesn't squash the leaves. Then tie the bag firmly around the base of the stem.
3 **Leave the plant in a sunny spot.**
4 **After an hour or two,** the inside of the bag will be covered with drops of water that the plant has "breathed out."

Striped celery

Try the coloring experiment at the left with a stick of celery. When you cut across the stem, the red dots show the "xylem," or tiny tubes that carry water and nutrients up from the roots.

Light tease

Plants turn their leaves and grow toward the light. Put a potted plant near a window and in a day or so you will see that all its leaves are facing the light. Then turn it around. How long does it take for the leaves to turn to face the light again?

Most plants grow fairly straight up toward the light, but what happens if the light is coming only from one side?

1 **Take a large cardboard box** and cut a wide slit out of the bottom of one side (see the picture).
2 **Plant a pot or tray of quick-growing seedlings,** like bean sprouts or young sunflowers.
3 **Put the box over the seedlings** so that no light gets in except through the slit.
4 **Put your experiment in a sunny place** with the slit facing the sun and leave it for a few days. What happens to the seedlings?
5 **You can tease them** by turning them around to face away from the slit. Put the box back in the sun and see what happens in the next few days.

Make an oxygen bubble

While leaves are making food, they also are making oxygen. In fact, much of the oxygen we breathe from the air has been made by plants. This experiment will show that plants give off oxygen.

1 **Buy a few aquatic plants** from a pet store that sells tropical fish.
2 **Fill an aquarium or a large glass or clear plastic container** with water and put the plants in the bottom. Put it in a sunny place.
3 **Cut off the top of a large, clear plastic bottle,** take off its screw cap, and place it over the plants.
4 **Balance a small glass over the top of the bottle** as shown in the picture. Make sure there is no air in the glass by holding it under water first.
5 **After a few days** you should notice a space at the top of the glass where oxygen is collecting. You may even see bubbles rising from the plants.

Wetlands

This habitat includes marshes, swamps, wet woods, and ditches, in addition to the banks and sides of ponds and streams. You will even find some of these flowers growing in shallow water that is still or slow-moving.

Most wetlands are free of trees and get a lot of sunshine. The flowers that bloom in wetlands usually need a lot of direct sunlight, and most of them bloom in the late spring and summer. Those that grow in swamps, however, have to cope with shade. They bloom earlier in the spring or are able to make do with less light.

All plants need water, but to survive in wet conditions the plants have to adapt in special ways. To prevent them from becoming water-logged, plants that grow in shallow water, like water lilies, have glossy, waterproof leaves and flowers. Most wetland plants have special air ducts in their leaves and stems to carry oxygen from the air to the parts of the plant growing underneath the surface.

Very wet soil is not as fertile as drier ground. Minerals and nutrients are easily washed away. The purple false foxglove, a plant in the figwort family, overcomes this problem by taking nourishment from the roots of certain trees onto which it clings. Water lilies take advantage of the water to disperse their seeds. This picture shows seven kinds of flowers from this section. How many can you identify?

Broadleaf arrowhead, broadleaf cattail, blue flag iris, spotted Joe-pye weed, marsh marigold, white turtlehead, white water lily

White Water Lily

These beautiful plants grow in quiet waters and ponds. The flowers open in the morning to show their many yellow stamens. The floating leaves are round, and they grow on long stalks from stems or rhizomes under the mud at the bottom of the pond. As the flowers die, their long stalks coil back under the surface so that the seed capsules ripen underwater. When they burst, the seeds rise to the surface and float away.

Water lily family
Flowers up to 8 in (20 cm) above the water
Flowers in May–July

Green Fringed Orchid

This plant grows in open swamps, bogs, wet woods, and meadows, and in marshes in the eastern half of Canada and the United States. The flowers are creamy-yellow or whitish-green. If you look closely, you can see that the lip of each is divided into three lobes. Each lobe is deeply cut and forms a fringe. The leaves are lance-shaped and grow upward on the lower part of the stem.

Orchid family
1–2 ft (30–61 cm) tall
Flowers in June–September

Stream Orchid

These showy flowers grow next to lakes, springs, and streams in the western United States, and form colonies of leafy stems that grow upward. Their leaves are large and lance-shaped or oval. The flowers are purple-veined, and grow from the base of the leaves. The sepals are greenish-brown. The pinkish or purplish petals are shorter. The purple lip is spoon-shaped with a salmon or pink tongue that moves when the flower is shaken. Because of that, it is often called chatterbox.

Orchid family
Up to 3 ft (91 cm) tall
Flowers in March–August

Broadleaf Cattail

This plant is easy to recognize from the long cylinder of brown flowers or seeds growing on thick stems with stiff, swordlike leaves. It grows in marshes and next to ponds and slow-moving rivers. A spike of tiny, yellow male flowers grow at the top of the stem above the brownish female flowers. The male flowers fade and disappear soon after shedding their pollen, leaving a bare stalk. The female flowers develop into brown seeds with a fluffy appearance when pulled apart. The rootstock was eaten by Native Americans and early colonists. It is also a favorite food of muskrats.

Cattail family—Up to 13 ft (4 m) tall
Flowers in May–October

Broadleaf Arrowhead

This plant grows in marshes, ditches, and next to lakes and slow-moving rivers. The arrowhead-shaped leaves are easy to recognize and give the plant its name. The many white or pale pink flowers grow in whorls near the top of the long, flowering stem. The plant is also called duck potato because of the potatolike swellings on its root. The swellings were a valuable food to the Native Americans, and you can still collect them between late summer and fall.
Water plantain family
Up to 4 ft (1.2 m) tall
Flowers in July–September

White Turtlehead

Look for the thick cluster of white flowers growing at the end of the stem. Turtleheads grow in wet places in eastern Canada and the United States. Each flower has two lips and looks something like a turtle's head. Look at the leaves, too. They are narrow and toothed, and grow in opposite pairs up the stiff stem.
Figwort family
1–3 ft (30–91 cm) tall
Flowers in July–September

Lizard's-tail

This plant grows in shallow water, swamps, and marshes in the eastern half of Canada and the United States. It gets its name from the tiny, white flowers that form long spikes, which droop at the tips like a lizard's tail. Look for the large, dark leaves, too. They are heart-shaped and are 3 to 6 inches (8 to 15 centimeters) long. The flowers are followed by juicy capsules.
Lizard's-tail family
2 to 5 ft (61–152 cm) tall
Flowers in June–September

Boneset

You may first see the spreading masses of grayish-white flower heads, but the best way to identify boneset is from its leaves. They are large, lance-shaped, wrinkled, and opposite to each other. The pair are joined so that the stem seems to grow through them. The hairy stems grow together in clumps. It grows in low, wet places in the eastern half of Canada and the United States. Boneset was used by the Native Americans, and later by the settlers, in herbal medicine as a tonic. The Native Americans used it to treat fevers associated with colds, influenza, and malaria, before the invention of modern drugs.
Daisy family
2–5 ft (61–152 cm) tall
Flowers in August–October

Wetlands

Canada Lily

This beautiful plant grows in the eastern United States in wet meadows and next to the edges of woods. It is also called wild yellow lily and meadow lily. Its drooping flowers are yellow or yellow-orange and marked with purplish-brown spots. The petals overlap to form a funnel, then arch backward at the end. The leaves are lance-shaped, and grow in whorls of between four and ten leaves.

Lily family
Up to 5 ft (1.5 m) tall
Flowers in June–August

Yellow-eyed Grass

Look for this grass beside ponds and ditches, in sandy swamps, and wet pine barrens, but only in the southeastern United States. This grass forms a clump of straight leaves with yellow flowers at the end of long, leafless stalks. The flowers rise from a cone of woody bracts which hides the buds and fruits. Each has three petals and three sepals. One sepal is hooded and soon drops off. The other two are boat-shaped or winged.

Yellow-eyed grass family
Up to 3 ft (91 cm) tall
Flowers in June–September

Marsh Marigold

Look for these showy, yellow flowers in marshes, wet meadows and thickets, and next to streams. The flowers have five to nine petals and as many as 100 stamens. Their stalks are hollow. The large, dark green leaves are heart-shaped and grow in clumps. Look for their toothed edges and long stalks, too.

Crowfoot family
Up to 2 ft (61 cm) tall
Flowers in April–May

Yellow Loosestrife

This plant grows in open swamps and wet places in the eastern United States. These bright yellow flowers form big, candlelike spikes. Look for the red spots on the petals. The leaves are opposite to each other and are canoe-shaped. Yellow loosestrife plants produce special buds at the base of the leaves. As the plants die in the winter, these buds drop to the ground and form new plants in the spring.

Primrose family
Up to 3 ft (91 cm) tall
Flowers in June–August

Seep-spring Monkey Flower

This plant grows all over the Rocky Mountains. For most of the year, it covers the ground with a mat of creeping, overlapping stems. Then in the summer, it sends up shoots with pairs of rounded leaves and yellow flowers spotted with orange. Look closely at one of the flowers. It has two broad lips that join to form a funnel. The upper lip has two lobes and the lower lip has three.
Figwort family
Up to 3 ft (91 cm) tall
Flowers in March–September

Sneezeweed

This plant grows in wet meadows, marshes, and ditches. It has a lot of yellow flower heads at the ends of the stem. They have a ball of greenish-yellow flowers in the center surrounded by a ray of yellow, drooping petals. These bend backward, so that the flowers look like round buttons with streamers attached to them. The toothed leaves are lance-shaped, and look like wings attached to the stems. This plant was used to make snuff, to make people sneeze.
Composite family
2–5 ft (61–152 cm) tall
Flowers in August–November
Also grown in yards

Pale Touch-me-not

This plant grows in wet, shady places in meadows and woods. The drooping, pale yellow flowers grow on long, arching stems from the base of the leaves. They have yellow petals and sepals that look like petals. Look closely and you might see a few red-brown spots on the yellow. The leaves are toothed and egg-shaped, and alternate up the stem. The flowers are replaced by green seed pods that, when ripe, burst and spread their seeds if you touch them. This plant is not as common as jewelweed (see page 49).
Balsam family
3–6 ft (91–182 cm) tall
Flowers in June–October

Yellow Water Lily

These yellow, bowl-shaped flowers grow in ponds and slow-moving streams in the western United States. They float on the water's surface or stand up above the water. The plant has two kinds of leaf: waxy, oval, notched leaves that float on the surface, and thin, delicate ones under the water. The flowers are followed by egg-shaped fruits that ripen above the surface and burst to release the seeds. The seeds can be roasted like popcorn or ground into meal.
Water lily family
Flowers 3–4 in (8–10 cm) above water
Flowers in April–September

Checkerbloom

These narrow, flowering spikes are crowded with deep pink flowers. They grow from a clump of round leaves with shallow lobes. Leaves higher up the stem are deeply divided into seven palmate lobes. The plants grow next to streams, ponds, springs, and in wet places on the lower slopes of the Rocky Mountains. Many kinds of checkerbloom are also grown as yard plants.

Mallow family
Up to 3 ft (91 cm) tall
Flowers in June–September

Snakemouth Orchid

You will easily recognize this flower, but you will be lucky to find it because it is quite rare. It grows in bogs in eastern Canada and the United States. The fragrant, pink flower has three pink sepals that look like petals, and two petals that arch over a flat lip. The lip is fringed and bearded with short, yellow-and-pink bristles. Each stem has one lance-shaped or oval leaf part of the way up. It is also sometimes called rose pogonia.

Orchid family
Up to 2 ft (61 cm) tall
Flowers in May–June

Cardinal Flower

You can't miss these spikes of brilliant red flowers. They grow mainly in wet places in the eastern half of the United States. Look closely at one of the two-lipped flowers. The upper lip stands up, but the lower one droops and spreads into three lobes. The leaves are narrow and toothed, and alternate up the stems that grow upward.

Lobelia family
2–5 ft (61–152 cm) tall
Flowers in July–September

Handsome Harry

This plant grows in bogs, damp meadows, and wet pinelands in the eastern and southern United States. You will easily recognize the flower because of its four large, pink petals and yellow stamens. Look for the fruit capsules that follow the flowers. They flare out at the neck and look like urns. The leaves are egg-shaped, and have almost no stalks. They grow in opposite pairs up the stem. It is also called Virginia meadow beauty.

Meadow Beauty family
1–2 ft (30–61 cm) tall
Flowers in July–September

Jewelweed

Look for this plant next to streams and springs, and in damp woods. Its large flowers are orange-yellow with reddish-brown spots. It is often called spotted touch-me-not. The flowers are helmet-shaped and hang in small clusters on long, arching stems from the base of the leaves. They are followed by capsules that burst open at the slightest touch. The stems are translucent and ooze a watery juice if broken. This juice and that of pale touch-me-not (see page 47), relieve the itching of poison ivy.

Balsam family
Up to 5 ft
(1.5 m) tall
Flowers in
June–October

Red Iris

This plant grows in swamp margins and wet grasslands in the eastern United States. The leaves are sword-shaped, and overlap in clumps at the base. The reddish-brown flowers grow at the ends of stems. The petals and sepals bend back and downward, leaving three arching red styles. It is also known as copper iris, because of the color of its flowers.

Iris family
About 3 ft (91 cm) tall
Flowers in April–May

Wetlands

Blue Flag Iris

Look for clumps of these violet or blue-violet flowers in the East in marshes, wet meadows, and on shores of ponds. The drooping sepals are darker blue. They are marked with yellow and white, with deep purple veins at the center. The three petals stand up. The overlapping, sword-shaped leaves sometimes stand up and sometimes arch. They grow from underground stems called rhizomes. These are poisonous, like those of many irises.

Iris family
Up to 3 ft (91 cm) tall
Flowers in May–August

Spotted Joe-pye Weed

These fuzzy, pinkish-purple flower heads look like ironweed, but they form more tightly packed, flat-topped clusters. Look for the lance-shaped, toothed leaves that grow in whorls of three to five leaves. Notice how the stout stems are streaked and spotted with purple. The plant grows in damp meadows, thickets, and on the banks of ponds.

Composite family
Up to 6 ft (1.8 m) tall
Flowers in July–September

Purple Loosestrife

You will easily spot large clumps of these purple or reddish flowers growing next to streams, lakes, and in marshes, wet meadows, and roadside ditches in the late summer. Look closely at the flower spikes, and you will see that they are made up of whorls of many flowers, each with six crumpled petals. The leaves are lance-shaped, and grow in opposite pairs.

Loosestrife family
2–4 ft (61–121 cm) tall
Flowers in May–July

Allegheny Monkey Flower

In the eastern United States, this flower grows next to streams and in marshes. It doesn't grow in western states. Look for the pairs of lance-shaped leaves and the blue flowers. Each flower has two lips with yellow at the center. Look for the square-shaped stem, too. The flowers are followed by capsules of seeds.

Figwort family
1–3 ft (30–91 cm) tall
Flowers in June–September

Purple False Foxglove

Growing on shores and in bogs, each of these pink flowers lasts only for one day. They are shaped a little bit like bells, and they grow in clusters at the ends of the wiry stems. The leaves are small and narrow and grow in opposite pairs. The plant is semi-parasitic, as it gets some of its food by attaching itself to the roots of certain trees.
Figwort family
1–4 ft (30–121 cm) tall
Flowers in July–September

American Speedwell

This plant grows in marshes and next to streams throughout much of Canada and the United States. The fleshy stems root in the mud, then creep and sprawl under the mud and send up new stems. Look for the open, oblong clusters of blue flowers, which grow from the base of the upper leaves. The leaves are lance-shaped and grow in pairs along the stems. It is also called American brooklime.
Figwort family
Up to 3 ft (91 cm) tall
Flowers in May–July

Woundwort

These purple flowers grow in whorls at the base of the upper leaves. Each flower has two lips. The upper one forms a hood, and the lower one is marked with white. The leaves are lance-shaped with jagged edges and grow in pairs up the stem. The plant grows in damp places and marshes. Woundwort is an antiseptic and was traditionally used to treat wounds. It supposedly stopped bleeding and helped the wound to heal.
Mint family
Up to 3 ft (91 cm) tall
Flowers in July–September

New York Ironweed

This plant has a lot of purple or deep lavender flower heads. It grows in low, wet places and on streambanks in parts of the Eastern United States. The toothed, lance-shaped leaves alternate up the erect stems. At one time ironweeds were used in herbal medicine to stimulate the appetite and help digestion.
Composite family
3–6 ft (91–183 cm) tall
Flowers in August–October

Preserving Wild Flowers

Most wild flowers soon wither if you pick them, but you can preserve them for a long time by pressing or drying them. Choose only flowers that you know are common, and do not pick them unless there are a lot of them. Remember to pick a stem with a leaf, or take a separate leaf to press with it.

Flat flower heads like buttercups, violets, Rocky Mountain columbine, wild flax, and prairie woodland-stars press well. Avoid very bulky flower heads like red clover, sunflowers, or teasel. It is better to dry those. Take a plastic bag to put the flowers in. It will help to keep them fresh until you get home.

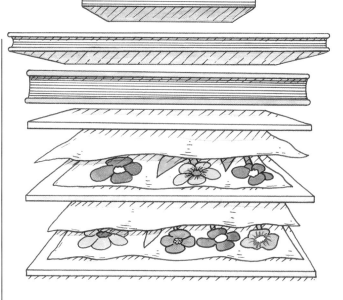

1 **Arrange the flowers and leaves carefully** on the sheets of paper towels. Give each flower enough room, and remember it will be preserved just as you have arranged it.
2 **Start with a piece of cardboard** or four layers of folded newspaper on a flat, hard surface. Lay a paper towel with flowers on top of it. Put another sheet of paper towel and then cardboard or folded newspaper on top of it.
3 **Keep adding layers of flowers** between paper towels and cardboard or newspaper until you have a stack no more than 6 inches (15 centimeters) high. Finish with a cardboard or newspaper layer.
4 **Carefully place the heavy books on top of the stack.**
5 **Leave the flowers for two weeks.** Then peel the paper back gently and check that the flowers are flat and dry. If they are not, leave them for another week.

Pressing flowers

You can buy a flower press ready-made, or you can make your own. You will need paper towels, cardboard or newspaper, and several heavy books. Choose a warm, dry room to place your press, and a table or cupboard where it can remain undisturbed for two or three weeks.

Drying flowers

Drying is even better than pressing for preserving wild flowers. It keeps their shape as well as their color, and in some cases dried flowers are hard to tell from fresh ones.

Members of the composite family, like daisies, thistles, and dandelions all dry well. Roses are good too. Always pick the flowers just before they are in full bloom.

Don't pick any flowers that are beginning to fade or wither, unless of course you wait until they go to seed. Poppies, teasels, and many other seed heads look very attractive dried. So do grasses.

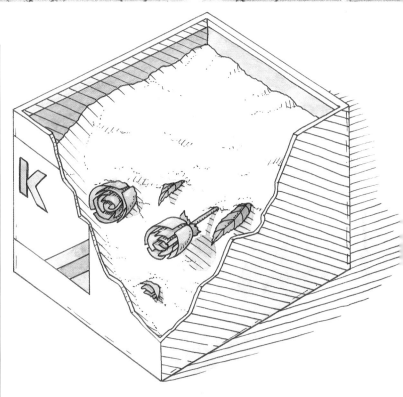

Air drying

The easiest way to dry flowers is by tying them into a bunch with a rubber band, then hanging them upside down in a dry, airy place for a few weeks. A linen closet is ideal because you can hang them up easily. An attic, spare room, or garage is also fine, but you will need to put up a pole or line from which to hang them. Don't put more than 8 to 10 stems into each bunch.

Drying more delicate flowers

Some flowers lose some of their shape and color if they are just air-dried. It's better to dry roses, lilies, and anemones using a mixture of cornmeal and borax, which you can buy from a grocery store. This drying method preserves leaves better, too.

1 **Find a box,** like a shoe box, that is large enough to hold the flowers easily.
2 **Mix equal parts of borax and cornmeal** together, enough to half fill the box.
3 **Pour some of the mixture into the box** to make a layer 1 inch (2.5 centimeters) deep.
4 **Cut the flower stems** so that they fit into the box, and carefully arrange the flowers on top of the mixture without overlapping each other.
5 **Gently sprinkle some more of the mixture over the flowers** until they are covered by a layer about 1 inch (2.5 centimeters) deep.
6 **After a week,** gently take the flowers from the box and dust off the drying mixture with an artist's paintbrush.

Deserts

The best word to describe a desert is dry, since deserts have less rain than anywhere else on Earth. And it is not hard to recognize a desert. If less than half the undisturbed ground is covered by plants, you are probably in a desert.

Desert plants have special ways of overcoming these extremely dry and often hot conditions. Plants usually lose water through their leaves, so the leaves of cacti have become no more than spikes. They store water inside their round, swollen stems. These stems have a limited surface for water to evaporate from. Other plants have long roots that grow close to the surface to catch as much moisture as possible.

The seeds of desert wild flowers sprout only when the rain comes, which, in North American deserts, is just once or twice a year. Then the seeds grow very quickly in the damp soil, and for a short while, the desert looks like it is covered with blooms. By the time the dry weather returns, the flowers have produced their seeds, which lie waiting for the next rainy season. This picture shows seven kinds of flowers from this section. How many can you identify?

Claret-cup cactus, fishhook cactus, desert lily, fringed twinevine, mountain phlox, California poppy, broom snakeweed

Tree Cholla

This cactus forms a shrub or small tree, with a lot of low branches. When the branches die they stay on the plant, so old plants are a mass of dead stems and new, green ones. The stems have very long joints. Look for the many round swellings with clusters of 10 to 30 short, yellowish spines. The flowers are dark reddish-lavender, or purple. They grow at the ends of the branches.
Cactus family
3–7 ft (91-213 cm) tall
Flowers in May–July
Also grows on plains and in pinyon-juniper woodlands

Claret-cup Cactus

This beautiful cactus is also called a hedgehog cactus because it forms a low mound of round spiny stems. Each stem has deep ribs covered with clusters of spines. The bright scarlet flowers are shaped like claret, or red wine, glasses and give the plant its name. They are followed by fat, red fruits.
Cactus family
2–12 in (5–30 cm) tall
Flowers in April–May
Also grows in dry mountain woods and on rocky slopes

Simpson Hedgehog Cactus

This cactus grows in clumps of ball-shaped stems. Each stem has 8 to 13 ribs with a lot of spiny swellings. Each cluster of spines has 5 to 11 thick spines in the center with 15 to 30 thinner, shorter spines around them. The flowers are rose-purple, white, or yellow-green. They grow near the top of the stem.
Cactus family
No more than 8 in (20 cm) tall
Flowers in May–July
Also grows among sagebrush and pinyon-juniper woodlands

Fishhook Cactus

Fishhook cacti have one or more round, single stems with many spines. The central spine of each cluster is shaped like a fishhook and is surrounded by straight, overlapping spines. The deep pink flowers grow in the spaces between the clusters of spines and are followed by smooth, red fruits.
Cactus family
Up to 6 in (15 cm) tall
Flowers in May–June
Also grows in very dry grasslands

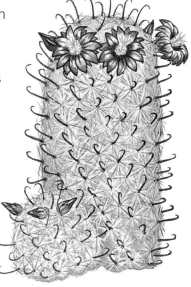

Deserts

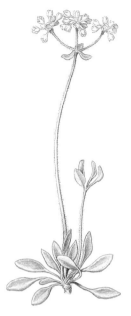

Sulphur Flower

These bright yellow flowers grow in clusters at the tops of long stalks. Look for the clump of leaves at the end of each branch. They are spoon-shaped with long stalks. They are more or less hairless above, but covered with white hairs underneath.
Buckwheat family
4–12 in (10–30 cm) tall
Flowers in June–August
Also grows on dry sunny areas from sagebrush deserts to tundra

Rabbitbrush

This shrub looks a lot like broom snakeweed (see opposite page). The yellow flower heads grow in thick clusters at the ends of the stems. The plant, which gives off a pleasant, strong odor, looks gray-white because its stems are covered thickly with gray or white hairs. The leaves are up to 3 inches (8 centimeters) long.
Composite family
Up to 7 ft (2.1 m) tall
Flowers in August–October

California Poppy

This plant is the state flower of California and is one of the best-known poppies. It has clumps of ragged, blue-green leaves, divided into deep segments. The orange-yellow flowers open only in sunlight. They close at night and stay closed on cloudy days.
Poppy family
Up to 2 ft (61 cm) tall
Flowers in February–October
Also grows on grasslands, hillsides, and in yards

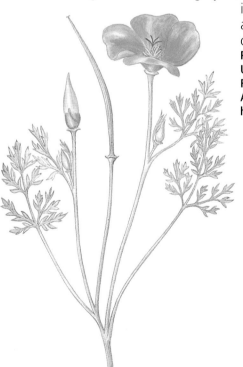

Threadleaf Ragwort

This plant grows in bushy clumps with branched stems and a lot of yellow flower heads. The long, thin leaves are bluish-green and covered in woolly hairs when they first grow. Threadleaf ragwort also grows well on ranges, but cattle usually avoid it because it is poisonous.
Composite family
1–3 ft (3–91 cm) tall
Flowers in April–September
Also grows on pinyon-juniper ranges and dry, rocky plains

Desert Prince's Plume

You can easily recognize this flower because of its long, spiky plumes of bright yellow flower heads. Look for the unusual shape of the small flowers. The yellow sepals bend backward as the flower opens and the four petals spread out, allowing the long stamens to stick far out of the flower. The flowers are followed by thin pods of seeds.

Mustard family
Up to 5 ft (1.5 m) tall
Flowers in May–July

Yellow Spiderflower

This tall plant grows on sandy flats and scrub, often near water. Look for the compound, palmate leaves with three to seven leaflets and the yellow flowers clustered at the top of the stems. The lower flowers open first and are followed by slender pods of seeds on arched, jointed stalks. Despite their strong, goaty smell, the flowers are very attractive to bees, so it is sometimes called bee plant.

Caper family
Up to 5 ft (1.5 m) tall
Flowers in May–September
Also found in juniper woodland

Broom Snakeweed

This plant has a lot of flat-topped, yellow flower heads and thin, brittle stems. The stems actually can be tied together to make a broom! Look for the plant's narrow leaves, and feel how sticky they are. Broom snakeweed was used by Native Americans as a remedy for snake bites.

Composite family
Up to 3 ft (91 cm) tall
Flowers in August–September

Golden Linanthus

This tiny plant has funnel-shaped flowers that vary in color from pale to deep yellow. Look for the purple-brown on their throats. The leaves are spaced apart on the thin stems, and each one has three to seven needlelike segments. Another popular name for this plant is desert gold.

Phlox family
Not more than 4 in (10 cm) tall
Flowers in May–June

Deserts

Fringed Twinewine

Look for this vine twining in and around the branches of other bushes. The white, purplish, or pink flower heads are made up of tiny starlike flowers. Each has five petals and a furry fringe. The leaves grow in pairs and are lance-shaped or triangular. It is also called climbing milkweed.
Milkweed family
Up to 10 ft (3 m) long
Flowers in April–August

Birdcage Evening Primrose

Several flowers, each having four white petals, grow from the top of each stem. They become reddish as they get older. Look at the leaves, too. They are toothed, and they grow in a rosette at the base of the stem. When the plant dies, its stems turn upward, forming what looks like a birdcage.
Evening primrose family
Up to 20 in (51 cm) tall
Flowers in May–July

Desert Lily

You can easily recognize this plant from its clumps of distinctive-looking leaves. They are long and narrow with wavy, crinkled edges. The white lilylike flowers are shaped like funnels, and they grow at the end of the flowering stem, which grows upward.
Lily family
1–6 ft (30–183 cm) tall
Flowers in March–May

Wild Heliotrope

The flowers of this plant grow in curled clusters. They uncurl as they open into very large blue flowers shaped like bells. The stems can grow upward or sprawl along the ground. The leaves are divided and look almost like ferns.
Waterleaf family—2–3 ft (61–91 cm) tall
Flowers in March–June—Also grows in fields

Desert Sand Verbena

This creeping plant has opposite, egg-shaped leaves and fragrant trumpet-shaped flowers. The flowers have rose-purple sepals that look like petals, and white centers. Feel the plant. It is covered with long, sticky hairs.
Vervain family
10 in (25 cm) high, 3 ft (91 cm) long
Flowers in March–October

Tuber Anemone

The flowers of tuber anemone can be white, rose-pink, or pinkish-purple, with yellow centers. The flowers don't have petals, but this isn't very noticeable because the sepals look just like petals. Each flower grows at the end of a separate branch with a whorl of three divided leaves midway on the stem and more at the base. The plant has tuberous roots in which it stores food and water.
Crowfoot family
4–6 in (10–15 cm) tall
Flowers in March–April

Purple Sage

You can recognize this plant because of the bright blue-violet flower clusters and the silvery leaves. The clusters are made up of whorls of two-lipped flowers surrounded by purplish bracts. The stems are spiny and form a broad, low-growing shrub.
Mint family
8–30 in (20–76 cm) tall
Flowers in May–July

Mountain Phlox

This little tufted plant has a lot of short, branched stems that grow from a woody base. Its flowers have five petals and can be lavender, pink, or white. The stems are thickly covered with narrow, gray-green, needlelike leaves. Rub them to see how strong they smell.
Phlox family
Up to 6 in (15 cm) tall
Flowers in May–July
Also grows in
western mountains

Things to Make

A flower calendar

You can make a flower calendar to put on your wall.

1 **Buy a large sheet of paper from an art supply store.** Divide the paper into 12 equal areas, or strips. Write the name of the months in the center of the strips.
2 **When you go for a walk,** make a note and a drawing of the flowers you see. If you have a camera, you could take a photo instead.
3 **Stick the photo or drawing onto the calendar** in the month you saw the flower.
4 **Alternatively, you can photocopy or draw the picture** of the flower from this book and color it before adding it to your calendar. Or you can cut a picture of the flower out of a nature magazine (with permission!).

For a more detailed record of the wild flowers you see, use a pad of plain paper. When you see a wild flower, make a drawing of it as shown (right). Write down the date you saw it and the place it was growing. Was it in bud, full flower, or in seed?

Use a new page for each kind of flower and allow space to add more notes from future walks. As your note pages build up, you can keep them in a ring binder.

Bookmark gift

Pressed tall, thin flowers make good bookmarks. You will need one sheet of clear adhesive-backed plastic.

1 **Cut two pieces of the plastic.** Make them a little bigger than you want the bookmark to be. Peel the backing off one piece of plastic and lay it sticky-side up on a flat surface.

2 **Lay the pressed flower carefully on the sticky plastic.**

3 **Peel the backing off the other cut piece** and lay it carefully on top of the flower. The two pieces do not need to match up exactly.

4 **Draw the outline of the bookmark onto the plastic** with a ballpoint pen and cut around it through both layers of plastic. The flower will show clearly from both sides of the bookmark.

Flower pictures

You can use dried flowers or pressed flowers (see pages 52–53) to make a picture.

1 **Use a piece of thick paper,** like artist's paper or good quality writing paper. Paint a landscape as a background, if you like.

2 **Arrange the flowers in a pattern,** or place them as they would look if they were growing. Don't put the flowers too close to the edge if you are planning to frame your picture.

3 **When you are happy with the arrangement,** stick it down using small amounts of glue on the back of each flower and leaf.

4 **If you have used pressed flowers,** you can frame your picture behind the glass. With dried flowers you will have to leave them uncovered.

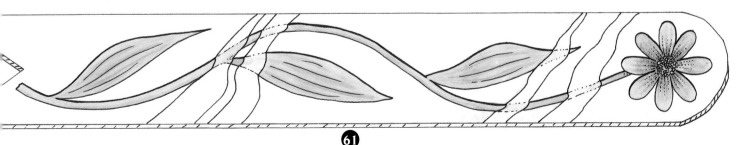

Roadsides & Parks

Many kinds of flowers grow along roadsides or railroad tracks, in parks or pastures, and on lawns or vacant lots. This section includes places where the natural habitat has been disturbed or altered by human activity.

Many of the plants in this habitat are not native to North America. They were brought here from other continents, mostly Europe and Asia. Some have escaped from yards, some from fields. Such starting points give these flowers particular problems, and the plants that adapt to human activity are the ones that thrive.

Many of these places have little fertile topsoil. The plants that grow there have to make do with fewer nutrients than in other habitats. Instead they need plenty of direct sunlight to thrive. Agricultural land has plenty of topsoil but, like vacant lots and building sites, the ground is only available for a short while. Plants that need a long time to establish themselves can't do well in these places. Instead, plants that can put down roots, grow, flower, and set seed quickly invade the land.

Many of these plants produce large numbers of seeds that can spread over a great distance. When the seeds land, the cycle can start over. The picture shows eight kinds of flowers from this section. How many can you identify?

Common burdock, chicory, red clover, white clover, oxeye daisy, common morning-glory, bull thistle, common yarrow

Roadsides & Parks

Pokeweed

This huge plant has long tapering leaves up to 12 inches (30 centimeters) long and reddish stems. You can't miss its strong, nasty smell. The flowers grow upward in spikes. Look carefully. They each have small stalks, greenish-white sepals, but no petals. They are followed by poisonous, dark purple berries.

Pokeweed family
Up to 10 ft (3 m) tall
Flowers in July–September
Also grows in open damp woods and clearings in Eastern States

Wild Strawberry

Wild strawberries are smaller, but sweeter and tastier, than cultivated strawberries. The white flowers have five, separate, round petals. Look into the center of the flower. The many pistils lead to a green cone, which will eventually swell to form the strawberry. If you look at a ripe strawberry, you can see the seeds embedded on the outside.

Rose family
Creeping stem with 3–6 in (8–15 cm) flower stalk
Flowers in April–June

Daisy Fleabane

The narrow ray flowers of the daisy fleabane are usually white, but they can be pink. They surround a wide, yellow center and grow in clusters at the end of the leafy stems. The leaves are toothed and lance-shaped. Both leaves and stems are covered with spreading hairs. Many kinds of fleabane have been developed as yard flowers.

Sunflower or daisy family
1–5 ft (30–152 cm) tall
Flowers in June–October
Also grows in yards and fields

Oxeye Daisy

You can tell the oxeye daisy apart from other daisies, because each stem has only one, large, daisylike flower head. The ray flowers are white, and the central disk is yellow and has a depression in the middle. Look at the leaves, too. They are dark green and have deep cuts. Oxeye daisies often grow together in large colonies. As a yard plant, it has a lot of other names, including moon daisy, Shasta daisy, and marguerite.

Composite family
Up to 3 ft (91 cm) tall
Flowers in May–August
Also grows in fields and yards

Common Mouse-ear Chickweed

Mouse-ear chickweeds get their name from their gray-green leaves, which are covered with short downy hairs and look like mice's furry ears. Each flower has five hairy sepals and five, deeply notched, white petals. The flowers grow in clusters at the ends of the flower stems. The rest of the plant creeps along the ground, putting down roots from time to time.

Pink family
Up to 12 in (30 cm) tall
Flowers in May–September
Also grows in lawns and fields

Common Yarrow

Look for the fairly flat clusters of small, white flower heads. Look for the soft, ferny, gray-green leaves, too. Yarrow has creeping, underground roots that often nurture large colonies. It has an aromatic smell and once was used to stop bleeding. American Indians used it to dress wounds and treat stomachaches.

Composite family
1–3 ft (30–91 cm) tall
Flowers in June–September
Also grows in fields

Pearly Everlasting

This plant is called everlasting because its dry, papery flowers last much longer than most flowers. Pearly everlastings are often used as dried flowers. The flower heads grow in branched clusters at the tops of stems. Look for the white, papery bracts around the yellow centers. It is these bracts that last so long. Look at the stem and narrow leaves, too—they are covered in white, woolly hairs.

Composite family
2–3 ft (61–91 cm) tall
Flowers in July–September
Also grows in yards and dry open places but not in the southern U.S.

Wild Carrot

You will easily see these large, flat umbels of creamy-white flowers. Look for the one purple or red flower in the center of each umbel. The leaves are fernlike, and alternate up the stem. When the flowers die, the umbels close up and look like birds' nests with many spiky fruits. Also known as Queen Anne's lace, it has swollen fleshy roots like cultivated carrots, but smaller, with a carroty smell.

Parsley family
1–3 ft (30–91 cm) tall
Flowers in May–October
Also grows in fields and meadows

Wild Mint

You can easily find this flower because of its strong smell. It often grows in fields of peppermint, but has to be weeded out because it ruins peppermint's flavor. The flowers are white, pale pink, or lavender, and grow in thick whorls from the bases of the leaf stalks of the upper leaves. The opposite leaves are oval and toothed. Look at the stems—some creep along the ground, others grow straight up.

Mint family
Up to 2 ft (61 cm) tall
Flowers in May–August
Also grows along streams
and in wet meadows

Bull Thistle

Thistles have spiny stems and spiny leaves. Even the swollen base of the flowers is covered with prickly bracts. The red-purple flower of the bull thistle is followed by a ball of fluffy, white seeds that blow away in the wind. The large leaves are lobed and tipped with spines. Look out for the spiny wings that run down the whole length of the stem as well.

Composite family
Up to 6 ft (1.8 m) tall
Flowers in May–August
Also grows in fields,
pastures and meadows

New England Aster

You may see this flower growing in yards or in tall clumps alongside streams. The purple flowers have yellow centers and grow on flower heads among the upper leaves. Feel how sticky the long flower stalks are. The leaves are lance-shaped, and alternate up the hairy stems.

Composite family
Up to 7 ft (2.1 m) tall
Flowers in July–October
Also grows in wet meadows
and swamps, mainly
in the central U.S.

Selfheal

As the name says, this plant was once used to help heal wounds and sore throats. It is hardly ever used as a medicine today, however. The blue-violet flowers grow in thick clusters at the tops of the stems. Look for their two lips and their hairy bracts. The leaves are egg- or lance-shaped, and are unevenly toothed. They grow in opposite pairs on short stalks.

Mint family
6–12 in (15–30 cm) tall
Flowers in May–September
Also grows in fields and lawns

Common Mallow

The common mallow has sprawling, branched stems covered with a lot of downy hairs. The flowers are white, veined, and tinged with pink or purple. They grow in clusters from the base of the long leaf stems. Look for the palmate leaves and for the fruits. Mallows are often called cheeses because each fruit looks like a round cheese cut into pieces.

Mallow family
Up to 2 ft (61 cm) tall
Flowers in April–October
Also grows in yards

White Clover

You can easily recognize white clover from its leaves, which are divided into three rounded leaflets. Look for the white band around the base of each leaflet. The thick, white or pink flower heads grow from the base of the leafstalk. All clovers are rich in nectar. Look for bees probing into the many small flowers that make up the flower head. Some of the best honey is made from clover.

Pea family
Up to 1 ft (30 cm) tall
Flowers in May–September
Also grows on lawns

Jimson Weed

By very careful of jimson weed. All parts of the plant are **very poisonous.** The seeds grow in prickly, egg-shaped capsules. The whole plant looks very coarse and gives off a strong odor. The white or violet petals of the flower form a long trumpet, the lower part of which is enclosed by the sepals. The leaves are large, egg-shaped, and lobed. The stem is coarse and purplish with many branches.

Nightshade family
Up to 5 ft (1.5 m) tall
Flowers in May–September
Also grows in pastures

Field Bindweed

Bindweed is easy to recognize. It is a creeping or climbing vine with pink or white flowers and arrowhead-shaped leaves. See how the five petals of each flower join together to make a funnel. Look for field bindweed straggling over the ground. You won't see the roots, but they go deep underground, up to 6 feet (1.8 meters) or more.

Morning-glory family
Creeping vine 3–10 ft (0.9–3 m) long
Flowers in May–August

Common Buttercup

You won't have any difficulty recognizing this well-known flower, which grows in grassy places. It has five, glossy yellow petals and a hairy stem that has many branches. Look at the leaves. They are divided and palmate. Most buttercups are slightly poisonous, and cattle and other grazing animals avoid them because of their burning, bitter taste.

Buttercup family
Up to 4 ft (1.2 m) tall
Flowers in May–September

Common Evening Primrose

These showy, yellow flowers open a few at a time and only in the evening. They close by noon the next day. Each flower has four petals and eight prominent stamens. Lance-shaped leaves with wavy, slightly toothed edges grow thickly on an erect, unbranched stem. The flowers are followed by large, oblong capsules that more or less stand up.

Evening primrose family
Up to 5 ft (1.5 m) tall
Flowers in May–August

Woolly Sunflower

You will easily recognize this plant with its many solitary, yellow flowers. Its leaves and stems look gray, because they are covered with gray-white, woolly hairs, which give the plant its name. The hairs help the plant retain water, enabling it to grow in dry, sunny places. The lower leaves are narrow and divided. The upper leaves are narrow, but not divided.

Composite family
Up to 2 ft (61 cm) tall
Flowers in May–August
Also grows in yards and dry places in Western States

Sticky Cinquefoil

This plant grows in open places in the Western States. Its yellow flowers grow in loose clusters at the ends of reddish flowering stems that grow upward. The stems grow in clumps and have special glands that make them sticky. The lower leaves are pinnate with five to nine toothed, egg-shaped leaflets.

Rose family
Up to 2 ft (61 cm) tall
Flowers in May–July

Golden Crownbeard

These flowers are bright yellow heads at the ends of long stalks. Look for the toothed, outer ray petals that grow around the yellow center. The toothed triangular leaves are gray-green. The stems have many branches and, if you look closely, you can see they are covered with tiny hairs. Golden crownbeard is also called cowpen daisy.
Composite family
Up to 5 ft (1.5 m) tall
Flowers in June–September
Also grows on ranges and pastures in Western States

Common St.-John's-wort

These little yellow flowers have five pointed petals and many stamens. Look closely at the petals, and you can see they have tiny, black dots around the edges. The leaves are narrow, canoe-shaped and grow in pairs. If you hold one of the leaves up to the light, you can see that it is covered by translucent dots.
St.-John's-wort family
15–30 in (38–76 cm) tall
Flowers in May–August
Also grows in meadows

Black Mustard

You will easily spot these bright yellow flowers, which add a splash of color to roadsides and fields. The lower leaves are large, bristly, and lobed. The upper leaves are smaller and toothed. The flowers are followed by long pods that press against the stem. In Europe, black mustard is farmed for its seeds, but in North America it is regarded as a weed. It is closely related to broccoli, cabbage, cauliflower, and Brussels sprouts.
Mustard family
Up to 6 ft (1.8 m) tall
Flowers in June–October
Also grows in fields

Dandelion

Dandelions are one of the best-known flowers. Look for their rosettes of wavy, lobed, and toothed leaves. The stalks are hollow, and the leaves ooze a milky juice if broken. The flower heads eventually wither into balls of parachuted seeds that scatter in the wind. The leaves can be eaten in salads, and the roots can be roasted and ground to make a coffee substitute.
Composite family
2–18 in (5–46 cm) tall
Flowers in March–September
Also grows on lawns and other grassy places, in fields and pastures

Bird's-foot Trefoil

Look for this bright yellow flower in grassy places and on roadsides. The flowers grow on long stalks from the base of a leaf. The leaves are divided into three small leaflets. The flowers yield to long pods that look like a bird's foot, but they are hard to find before they twist and split open to release the seeds.

Pea family
Up to 2 ft (61 cm) tall
Flowers in May–August
Also grows in fields

Yellow Salsify

These showy, pale yellow flowers are easy to find. Look for the long, slender, green bracts that protect the flowers when they are closed and extend beyond the ray flowers when they are open. Look at the stems, too. They swell just below the flower heads. If you break a stem, milky juice oozes out. The flower heads eventually wither into large, spectacular balls of feathery parachutes, each one attached to a seed.

Composite family
12–30 in (30–76 cm) tall
Flowers in May–September
Also grows in dry, open places

Common Toadflax

You will see this bright cluster of yellow-and-orange flowers easily. Also called butter and eggs, the plant forms large colonies of leafy stems that grow upward, as well as yellow spikes of flowers. Look carefully at the flowers. Each has two lips with a straight spur at the bottom of the flower and is orange inside. In herbal medicine, the plant was used to treat jaundice. If it is soaked in milk, it also makes a good fly poison.

Figwort family
1–2½ ft (30–76 cm) tall
Flowers in May–October
Also grows along railroads and in dry fields

Canada Goldenrod

You can't miss the long, glowing yellow plumes of this flower. It grows in woodland clearings and open places, except in the southern United States. The plumes are made up of masses of tiny flowers that grow on many short, arching branches at the tops of the stems. The tall stems, which grow upward, sway in the wind and are covered with many lance-shaped leaves that alternate up them.

Composite family
Up to 5 ft (1.5 m) tall
Flowers in May–November

Tansy

These yellow flower heads are easy to recognize. They are composed of tiny disk flowers and a few or no ray flowers. These grow in flat-topped clusters on branches of small stalks. The stems are straight and strong and the alternate leaves are soft and divided into fernlike, toothed segments. Tansy was used to heal sprains and bruises. It also repels insects that don't like its bitter smell.
Composite family
2–3 ft (61–91 cm) tall
Flowers in July–September
Also grows in fields

Common Mullein

This tall, sturdy plant has long, yellow spikes of flowers and unusual leaves. It grows well in dry places because the leaves channel rainwater down the stems and into the roots. The leaves are also covered with woolly down that stops them from drying out. People have used the leaves for rouge, as shoe liners, mixed in tobacco, and as a remedy for chest diseases.
Figwort family
Up to 6 ft (1.8 m) tall
Flowers in May–August
Also grows in fields

Black-eyed Susan

You won't miss these showy flowers with orange-yellow rays and dark-colored centers. Each flower head is 2 to 3 inches (5 to 8 centimeters) across. Feel the leaves. They are rough with coarse hairs. They vary in shape and can be lance-shaped, oval, or egg-shaped, with or without teeth.
Composite family
1–3 ft (30–91 cm) tall
Flowers in June–October
Also grows on hillsides, prairies, fields, and in open woods in southern Canada and most of the U.S.

Day Lily

These tawny-orange flowers are shaped like a funnel and grow in clusters at the ends of long, bare stems. The bright green leaves are shaped like broad blades of grass, and they grow together in clumps at the base of the plant. Day lilies are well-known yard plants, but many have escaped to grow wild on roadsides and in meadows. They were originally brought to North America from Japan.

Lily family
Up to 5 ft (1.5 m) tall
Flowers in May–July
Also grows in yards

Butterfly Weed

This plant gets its name because its orange flowers attract many butterflies. Each flower has five back-curving petals and a five-part central crown. Look for them in large umbels near the tops of the leafy stems, which grow upward. They are followed by large pods of hairy seeds. This plant is also called pleurisy root and was used in Native American and herbal medicines to treat pleurisy, bronchitis, pneumonia, whooping cough, and other chest diseases.

Milkweed family
Up to 30 in (76 cm) tall
Flowers in May–August
Also grows in dry open fields, meadows, and prairies in the eastern, midwestern, and southern U.S.

Red Clover

To tell red clover apart from white clover with a pink flower (see page 67), look at the leaves. Red clover has a light V-shaped pattern on the leaflets. The purplish-red flower clusters grow between two leaves at the ends of the stems. Clover petals stay on the flower head after they have withered. Look then for the seed pods in the brown flower heads.

Pea family
Up to 2 ft (61 cm) tall
Flowers in May–September
Also grows in fields

Fringed Redmaids

You will easily see these small but brilliant, bright rose-red flowers. The plant has several spreading stems and narrow leaves. The leaves are fleshy, telling you that this plant is a succulent. You will find it growing in grassy places in the western United States, where there is water early in the year.
Purslane family
4–16 in (10–41 cm) tall
Flowers in April–May

Carolina Rose

It is easy to tell that this flower is a rose. Also called pasture rose, it has five heart-shaped, pink petals and a lot of stamens in the center. The arching stems are protected by stiff hairs and straight thorns. The compound leaves are divided into three to seven oval leaflets. The flowers are followed by bright red fruits called hips. Rose hip syrup, jelly, and tea are made from them, and they are rich in vitamin C and minerals.
Rose family
Up to 3 ft (91 cm) tall
Flowers in April–June
Also grows in grasslands and dry woods in Eastern States

Pimpernel

You will only see these attractive red or orange flowers fully open on bright, sunny mornings. They close at about 3:00 p.m., and stay closed in cloudy weather. Look for the sprawling stems and pointed, egg-shaped leaves that grow in opposite pairs. Look for the seed capsules, too. They have hinged lids that open to release the seeds.
Primrose family
Low-growing, 4–12 in (10–30 cm) tall
Flowers in June–August
Also grows in sandy places

Lady's-thumb

You will find this plant almost everywhere on damp, cultivated land and desolate ground. Its many pink flowers grow in thick spikes at the ends of the stems, which grow upward. Look at the leaves, too. They are small and lance-shaped with a dark green triangle on each one.
Buckwheat family
8–32 in (20–81 cm) tall
Flowers in June–September

Roadsides & Parks

Spotted Knapweed

At first glance, knapweeds look a lot like thistles, but they don't have spines or prickles. You can tell spotted knapweed apart from the other knapweeds by looking at the swollen base under the pink-purple flower head. It is spotted with black-tipped bracts. The stem is branched and wiry, and the long, narrow leaves are divided into segments.
Composite family
2–4 ft (61–121 cm) tall
Flowers in June–August
Also grows in fields and pastures in Eastern States

Teasel

Teasels grow in wet places. They have upright, prickly stems and prickly leaves. The lower leaves join across the stem, making a cup to collect water and drown insects that might attack the plant. The tiny pale purple flowers grow together in a cone-shaped head. The flowers in the center open first and new ones open daily toward the top and bottom, forming two bands that move in opposite directions. Look for the dead, dried flower heads right through the winter.
Teasel family
Up to 6 ft (1.8 m) tall
Flowers in July–October

Smooth Aster

Look for the smooth aster's purple flowers with yellow centers. The stems and leaves are smooth and often look grayish. The narrow leaves alternate up the stems. See how the base of the leaves seem to grip the stem.
Composite family
Up to 4 ft (121 cm) tall
Flowers in April–July
Also grows in dry, open places in eastern Canada and U.S.

Common Morning-glory

Morning-glory is really a tropical plant. It was brought here from tropical America as a yard plant. The funnel-shaped flowers can be blue, purple, pink, or white. They grow from the base of the leaves that are broad and heart-shaped. The stems form a twining vine, and if you look closely you can see they are covered in hairs.
Morning-glory family
Creeping vine up to 10 ft (3 m) long
Flowers in July–October
Also grows in fields, thickets, and yards in the Eastern States

Common Burdock

The pink or lavender flowers peep out of the top of the swollen base. Look for the hooked bracts that cover the base. The flowers are followed by hooked burs that cling to animals' fur and to clothes. Look at the leaves, too. They have long, hollow stalks and are typically heart-shaped, particularly lower down the stem. The reddish stems form a bushy plant with many branches.

Composite family
About 5 ft (1.5 m) tall
Flowers in May–August
Also grows in fields

Crown Vetch

This small, straggling plant was brought to North America as a yard plant but has escaped into the wild and grows in grassy places. Look for the round clusters of pink flowers on long flower stalks that grow from the base of the leaves. The compound leaves have 15 to 25 leaflets each. Look for the upright seed pods that follow the flowers.

Pea family
1–2 ft (30–61 cm) tall
Flowers in May–August

Common Milkweed

Look at the top of the stem for the drooping clusters of dull purplish flowers that grow from the base of the leaf stems. Each flower has five back-curved petals and a five-part crown that grows upward. They are followed by large, upright pods of seeds attached to hairy parachutes. The leaves are opposite, oblong, and covered with downy hairs underneath. The stems of milkweeds contain a poisonous milky juice.

Milkweed family
Up to 6½ ft (2 m) tall
Flowers in June–August
Also grows in fields in the eastern and midwestern U.S.

Fireweed

This flower grows very quickly in places that have been burned. It sends out creeping, underground stems to form large colonies of bright pink or rose-purple flowers. The flowers open from the bottom first and form long spikes. Look for the narrow purple sepals behind the broad petals. The flowers yield to very noticeable seeds. They are attached to long, silky hairs that blow away in the wind.

Evening primrose family
Up to 6 ft (1.8 m) tall
Flowers in June–August
Grows in burned or recently cleared areas

Bachelor's-buttons

These deep blue flower heads are hard to miss. The leaves are narrow and the stems are slender and wiry and grow upward. Look carefully at the flower heads. The blue disk flowers are tubular. Underneath the flower head is the hard, round seedbox, covered with fringed bracts. This flower, when grown in yards, can also be pink or white.
Composite family
Up to 3 ft (91 cm) tall
Flowers in May–August
Also grows in fields and yards

Bluebell of Scotland

This nodding, bell-shaped flower is easy to see, because it grows on such sparse land. You may see it all the way across Canada, in northern U.S. states, and in the western mountains. Look for the narrow leaves and five joined petals. This delicate flower has many other names—fairy bells, harebell, lady's thimbles, and also sheep bells because it often grows where sheep like to graze.
Bellflower family
Up to 15 in (38 cm) tall
Flowers in June–September
Also grows on dry grasslands, cliffs, and rocky areas

Common Periwinkle

The common periwinkle does not grow very high, so you might have to look carefully for its small, bright blue flowers among the other plants. The five petals all curve the same way, so the flower looks like a wheel with a white hub at the center. The leaves are dark green and grow opposite each other. Periwinkles were originally brought from Europe as yard flowers.
Dogbane family
Up to 7 in (18 cm) high
Flowers in April–May
Also grows in yards and borders of woods

Bluet

These little, sky-blue flowers have yellow centers and grow at the end of thin, straight stalks. The small, oval leaves grow up the stalk in opposite pairs. Look for the larger leaves at the bases of the stems.
Madder family
3–6 in (8–15 cm) tall
Flowers in April–June
Grows in lawns, meadows, and fields in the Eastern States

Asiatic Dayflower

This low, sprawling plant is easy to recognize because of its flowers. Each small flower has two large blue petals and one smaller whitish one. The leaves are lance-shaped and alternate up the stem.
Spiderwort family
1–3 ft (30–91 cm) long
Flowers in June–October
Also grows in borders of woodlands in the Eastern States

Chicory

The bright blue flowers of chicory are easy to see, even from a moving car. If you can, look for the rosette of wavy, toothed leaves at the base of the stalk. The young shoots can be eaten raw in salads or cooked as a vegetable. In Europe, its roots are roasted and ground, and added to coffee or drunk instead of coffee.
Composite family
Up to 5½ ft (1.6 m) tall
Flowers in May–August
Also grows in fields

Common Spiderwort

You may not see the common spiderwort's blue or purple flowers immediately. They can be hidden by the bracts, which are longer and wider than the leaves. The plant grows in clumps of tall stems which grow upward, but they are hidden by the long, interlocking leaves, as well.
Spiderwort family
Up to 2 ft (61 cm) tall
Flowers in April–July
Also grows in damp woodlands and meadows, mainly in the South

Find Out More

Glossary

annual: plant that dies after one year

anther: knob at the top of the stamens that contains pollen

biennial: plant that dies after two years

bulb: thick, roundish underground structure that stores food in certain plants

florets: tiny disk or ray flowers that are packed into a composite flower head (a flower head made of many tiny flowers)

leaflets: small leaves that are grouped together to form one big leaf

lobed: leaf that has its edges deeply divided

nectar: sugary liquid produced by flowering plants and eaten by insects and birds

ovary: part of the stigma where the egg cells are produced

ovule: egg cell; in plants, it develops into the seed

palmate: leaf that has lobes or leaflets all coming from one central point

perennial: plant that lives for several flowering seasons

pinnate: leaf that has several lobes or leaflets arranged directly across from each other on the sides of a stem

pollen: powdery substance from the anthers that fertilizes (unites with) the egg cells in the ovary

pollination: when pollen is carried (such as by wind or insects) from the anthers to the stigma

rhizome: underground stem that can produce leaves and flowers that rise above the surface; it can also store food in some plants

seed: fertilized egg (egg cell that has united with pollen) of a flower

sepal: green, leaflike part that protects a bud and later grows around the base of the flower

stamen: male part of the flower; at the top are the anthers

stigma: female part of the flower; it contains the style and ovary

stomata: tiny holes in leaves that allow a plant to breathe—carbon dioxide, oxygen, water vapor, and other gases pass into and out of the leaves through the stomata

style: tube in the stigma through which the pollen travels to the ovary

succulent: plant with thick, fleshy leaves or stems full of juice

tuber: thick part of an underground stem from which new plants can grow

whorl: group of leaves that grows at the same level around the stem

xylem: tiny tubes that carry water and food from the roots to the leaves of a plant

Organizations

The **American Association of Botanical Gardens and Arboreta** is the best source of information about U.S. botanical gardens. While not wild habitats, botanical gardens provide an excellent opportunity to see rare species of wild flowers and other plants. Contact: American Association of Botanical Gardens and Arboreta, 100 W. 10th Street, Suite 614, Wilmington, Delaware 19801; (302) 655-7100. http://www.aabga.org

The **Lady Bird Johnson Wildflower Center** is one of the best beginning points for wild flower buffs. The center publishes a variety of material with information on wild flowers and organizations throughout North America. Contact: Lady Bird Johnson Wildflower Center, 4801 La Crosse Avenue, Austin, Texas 78739; (512) 292-4100. http://www.wildflower.org

Many of the preserves owned by the **Nature Conservancy** and its chapters conserve unique and threatened wild flower habitats. Contact: Nature Conservancy, Suite 100, 4245 North Fairfax Drive, Arlington, Virginia 22203-1606; (800) 628-6860. http://nature.org

The **North American Native Plant Society** publishes one of North America's foremost native plant magazines, *Wildflower*. Write to: North American Native Plant Society, P.O. Box 84, Station D, Etobicoke, Ontario M9A 4X1. http://www.nanps.org/index.shtml

Index

Additional Resources

A Field Guide to Medicinal Plants and Herbs of Eastern and Central North America Steven Foster and J. A. Duke (Houghton Mifflin, 2000).

A Field Guide to Western Medicinal Plants and Herbs Steven Foster and Christopher Hobbs (Houghton Mifflin, 2002).

National Audubon Society Field Guide to North American Wildflowers: Eastern Region John W. Thieret and others (Knopf, 2001).

National Audubon Society Field Guide to North American Wildflowers: Western Region Richard Spellenberg (Knopf, 2001).

The Nature and Science of Flowers Jane Burton and Kim Taylor (Gareth Stevens, 1998).

Wildflowers (National Geographic Society, 2002)

Wildflowers of North America Frank D. Venning (Golden Press, 1984).

Index